The Monocle Book of HOMES

The Monocle Book of
HOMES

A guide to inspiring residences

First published in the United Kingdom in 2021 by
MONOCLE and Thames & Hudson Ltd,
181A High Holborn, London, WC1V 7QX

First published in the United States of America in 2021 by
MONOCLE and Thames & Hudson Inc,
500 Fifth Avenue, New York, New York, 10110

MONOCLE is a trading name of Winkontent Limited

© 2021 Winkontent Limited of Midori House,
1 Dorset Street, London, W1U 4EG

British Library Cataloguing-in-Publication Data
A catalogue record for this book is available from
The British Library

Library of Congress Control Number: 2020951860

For more information, please visit *monocle.com*

To find out more about new Thames & Hudson releases,
exclusive content and author events, visit
thamesandhudson.com
thamesandhudsonusa.com
thamesandhudson.com.au

Edited by *Nolan Giles & Joe Pickard*
Foreword by *Tyler Brûlé*

Designed by *Monocle*
Proofreading by *Monocle*
Typeset in *Plantin & Helvetica*

Printed by *Graphicom*

Printed and bound in Italy

ISBN 978-0-500-97114-7

This book was printed on paper certified
according to the standards of the FSC®

Contents

1

The homes

Whether you dream of owning a
cosy cabin or a mid-century apartment
(or perhaps are lucky enough to have one
already) you'll find plenty of inspiration
in our tour of 20 standout residences
from Lebanon to Indonesia.

2

Essays

No two homes are the same – nor should
they be. We ask a few top writers and
designers to reflect on their own living
spaces and highlight the small things they
believe make a big difference.

3

Community

Home extends far beyond the front door,
so we thought it apt to explore the modern
art of living together. We highlight the
community-driven urban developments
and neighbourhoods that tick all the boxes.

4

Greenery

If you haven't already, it's time to put
down some roots – literally. As urban
spaces welcome foliage back into the fold,
learn how you can fill your home and
garden with wellbeing-boosting plants.

5

Materials

When it comes to building a home, which
materials should you use? We review six
construction classics and showcase how
to get the best out of each of them.

6

Details

Get up close and personal with the
details that make our dwellings distinct.
Snapped by MONOCLE's photographers
and editors, here's our personal scrapbook
of inspiration.

7

Designs for living

From chairs and lamps to kettles, clocks
and calendars, this is our edit of the 100
failsafe items that will help make your
house a home.

Foreword
Room to grow

Welcome and come on in. We've laid out quite the spread for you this time around (or 132 to be precise), made everything comfortable and considered so that you can linger for hours.

And to make this whole exercise extra entertaining we've invited 100 of our favourites from the design world to keep you company as you ponder life's big questions. Which chair would make the most sense for my balcony? (We'd suggest something from Fiam.) What brand does a good job of creating timeless, dependable sofas and armchairs that are easy on the eye? (Søren Lund for sure.) And how about a dining table that can host the odd craft session on a Sunday and a bit of Monday morning conference-calling? (Nikari can definitely sort you out on this front.)

As you meander through these pages you'll note that our editors, writers and photographers haven't just taken you around the world, they've also come up with a series of residences that chronicle more than 15 years of MONOCLE reportage. We've compiled some of the best examples of fine architecture, lasting craftsmanship and places that epitomise the personalities of their owners and collaborators. After a year that saw many of us spend perhaps more time within our residences than we might like, we wanted to throw open the doors, peer over garden walls, wander across courtyards and take in the views from some of our favourite cities, best bits of coastline and cosiest villages.

As this book was being reviewed and scrutinised on the desks and floors of our Zürich office a visitor asked me, "What makes a MONOCLE home? What is the criteria that allows a residence to make the cut?" A good question and it took me a while to gather my thoughts as I was busy swapping pictures around. "It needs to feel like it has lived a little," I explained. It should have seen years of lazy Saturday mornings, it needs a few dents and scratches, the owners should have a passion for collecting and it should never, ever, ever feel like it was 'decorated'. Rather it should feel like

it still has room for one more sideboard, a few extra paintings, the right set of lamps and maybe some pillows from Johanna Gullichsen.

Of course the best apartment or villa isn't worth much if it's not connected to its surroundings or offering up a proper sense of community, so we've also devoted ample space reminding ourselves, developers and architects what makes a great neighbourhood tick and why there are some essentials that shouldn't be missed when planning from scratch or considering a purchase.

We hope this latest edition from our imprint goes beyond pure inspiration and that you manage to meet a new designer to help you figure out your kitchen, find a couple of modernist pots to make your palms look perkier and maybe an architect (or two) who you can commission to build a little compound that hosts multiple generations. Enjoy.

Tyler Brûlé
Editorial Director
& Chairman

Introduction
Home truths

Step right in ⟶

What makes a house a home?
Address to impress

Our homes are the backdrop to our daily lives, the moments both momentous and mundane. They are the places that sustain us, inspire us and put us at ease; spaces where we seek solitude and host our friends and family. But for such an important idea, "home" as a concept is broad and fluid. It starts with the walls that enclose us as we slumber at night but extends to the neighbourhood far beyond our actual doorstep. It's in the things and people that surround us but it's also changeable and flexible. Ultimately it is something that can be packed up in boxes and moved wholesale to somewhere completely new. These are the ideas that MONOCLE has celebrated when covering residences in its design and architecture pages and *The Monocle Book of Homes* addresses this in the largest of senses – the tangible and the intangible. Hopefully this tome will spark thoughts, debates and make suggestions to help you create better places for living.

We open with a selection of residences that we believe have got the balance right. This chapter takes you from Athens to Brisbane (past Los Angeles, Jakarta and rural Japan) to offer inspiration for your own home, whether that's a pied-à-terre in the city or a rambling rural estate. This joyful anthology of beautiful spaces is packed with great photography that we think delivers the bigger picture, as well as a focus on the smallest of details.

Next we invite a team of key thinkers, writers and designers to share some home truths in a series of essays, covering everything from the design of a chair to how a house isn't a home unless it has a dog that barks every time the doorbell rings. We go on to explore the impact of good design more broadly – how clever architecture, urban planning, interior design and the furniture that we fill our homes with can have a life-enhancing impact. This could mean a humble balcony that provides a glimpse of the great outdoors or something more complex like how a housing block's architecture can ensure both a sense of privacy and space for meaningful interaction with neighbours.

Finally, we look at how it's often the smallest things that make the greatest difference and offer some advice on ways to kit out your home – our inventory of 100 great fittings, fixtures and furniture pieces can get you on the right track. We even slip on a gardening glove and get to grips with how a well-tamed vegetable patch can make us more content.

Good homes are places where lives can unfold – they are the environments that reflect our personalities. At home, we're able to have authorship over the way we live, through the choices we make when building and furnishing our spaces (not to mention the bits we leave well alone). With this in mind, we hope this book inspires you to make your home that little bit happier, healthier or more hospitable. It's a modest aim but it may just change your life.

1. The afternoon light creates patterns on the walls of this Los Angeles home 2. Taking a break on a leafy roof terrace in Milan 3. A dappled spot in Long Beach, California 4. Geometric balconies of the Park Towers development in Bogotá

1 2

3 4

The homes
Come on in

Join us for a tour of 20 residences that we would be happy to call home – from a timber-clad treasure in rural Finland to a sun-splashed apartment in Mexico City. Knock knock.

Even the best homes aren't ever really "perfect", as much as they are perfect reflections of those who reside in them. Rarely does a single resident or architect commission an ideal, ready-made abode – creating a house takes time. In this chapter we spin the yarns of 20 handsome homes, highlighting their histories and influences, their construction and the finishing touches while unveiling the processes through which many people forged them. We picked residences that resonated with us – some for their elegance and attention to detail, others for their more humble and homely charms.

From a terraced townhouse in an English city to a converted cottage on a Tasmanian island, no two projects are alike. But there is a common thread that links them in the quality of the design and overall ambition to improve the daily lives of those occupying them. This is not grandiose, statement architecture – this is sensible design delivered with empathy, which offers the occupier comfort. A dose of luxury doesn't go amiss here and there either. Yet it's a richness that comes in many forms – be it the placement of clever openings to allow a subtropical breeze to bless a suburban Aussie house or the sliding doors of a Spanish retreat that make the most of the stunning views. Some of these homes, like an off-grid cabin in Portugal, sink seamlessly into the landscape. Others, like a private greenery-draped hideaway in Jakarta, form an oasis from the noisy environment outside. But all of these homes provide a true sense of place. So let's creak open the door and delve inside.

Architect Sandy Cavill renovated his parents' Brisbane home with
a respect for the past, the city and nature – and his folks, of course.

1
The subtropical sanctuary
Brisbane, Australia

In 2014, Brisbane-born-and-bred architect Sandy Cavill took on a commission from the most exacting of clients: his own parents. Much more than a straight conversion, the prewar wooden worker's cottage in the leafy suburb of New Farm required an understanding of the city's unique subtropical climate and the context of an ever-changing Australian suburban vernacular.

Common to Brisbane, this particular housing stock had been occupied by postwar Italian immigrants who had set about adapting the cottages to their own tastes. Their efforts often involved covering the timber homes in concrete render and bricking up the lower parts of the cottages, originally built on stilts for ventilation and protection from the elements. Such efforts to "Mediterraneanise" the houses haven't always been successful but when the opportunity arose for Cavill to work on one he decided to put his own spin on these homespun alterations. "We thought, 'Why don't we have a go at legitimising the process and extending this Mediterraneanised architecture in a considered way'," he says.

The language of these upgrades is referenced directly in the renovation: Cavill added an extension of wood and concrete, replicating the rough-to-the-touch render of nearby homes while making the transition between cottage and extension as fluid as possible.

1

2

1. A leafy entrance 2. A bridge structure supports the new extension allowing fresh air to circulate 3. Vine-covered garden walls provide privacy from neighbouring houses 4. A sunny spot on the sofa 5. Family dog Cookie is a little camera-shy 6. Taking a break in the living room

3 4

5 6

1

1. Sliding glass doors open onto a sun-dappled courtyard at the centre of the house, providing almost every room with a view of the foliage-filled area

Architect:
Renovation by
Cavill Architects.

Year built:
Built in the late 19th
century, the property
was extended in 2014.

Size:
The site is 438 sq m.

Key materials: Wet
dash render, Venetian
lime plaster, concrete
and timber.

**What makes the
property unique:**
Its contemporary layout
that goes beyond an
open-plan space.

**The architect's
favourite element:**
"The house offers my
parents the sanctuary
and privacy they had
previously sought
elsewhere."

1. A view of the pared-back kitchen 2. The patina of the external, untreated wooden pergola will develop over time 3. Smart fittings 4. Artek's Stool 60 provides a hint of colour in the bathroom 5. Light bounces around the mirror-clad, all-white room 6. Sunny workstation 7. Cookie gets a good pat

1

2

3

4

5

6

7

"The timber in the new portion is intended to be expressive, akin to the materiality and detailing of the original timber cottage," says Cavill.

The extension was conceived as a sort of ruin emerging from the tropical landscape, with walls left looking fragmented and plant tendrils snaking up surfaces and hanging from the ceiling. The expansive sliding doors open it up to the elements while a central courtyard creates extra breathing room. Sunlight bounces off the walls, filling the area with dappled light. The crowning glory, though, is the flat roof which is planted with colourful shrubbery. "The intent is that nature will eventually engulf it. The external timber is unprotected so its age and patina will enable the building to recede further into the vegetation."

The house succeeds in creating a sense of sanctuary: the concrete walls' shapely recesses face skywards while most windows point to the privacy of the courtyard or garden. Luckily for Cavill, his parents were trusting clients. "They simply chose not to impose their ideas. In the end, it exceeded anything they could have imagined."

*While a life's worth of travelling has informed this South Tyrolean haunt,
the owners have also found inspiration on their doorstep – to charming effect.*

2
The mountainside renovation
Merano, Italy

Architect:
Originally designed
by Danilo Menia;
renovation overseen
by Harry Thaler.

Year built:
1960s

Size:
300 sq m

Key materials:
Swiss pine, brick,
stone, concrete
and marble.

**What makes it
unique:** Its sensitive
transformation from
a block of flats to
a comfortable,
light-filled home.

1

When the owners discovered a small, pastel-pink apartment block of three units in Merano, set back from the town and the Passer River, they were won over by the property's location and strong modernist bones. The building – a brick, stone, concrete and marble 1960s gem – promised the perfect renovation project and the pair purchased it in 2012.

In less than six months, their vision for a gentle transformation was devised by architect Harry Thaler, whose work for the regional food retailer Pur Südtirol had caught their eye. A team supervised by master builder Martin Mitterer added sliding timber screens to divide the home, transformed upstairs kitchens into sunny living spaces and smartened the exterior with cool-grey paint.

Today, it's difficult to imagine it being anything other than the handsome balcony-blessed, three-storey home it is now. Swinging open a decorative 1960s

wrought-iron gate, visitors are greeted by a neat garden that runs the length of the house. It is Japanese in spirit but its verdant subtropical nature – alive with floppy ferns and tall imported monkey puzzle trees – reflects the comfortable living that this warm corner of the Dolomites offers.

On the bright tiered lawn, colourful Swiss café outdoor seating and a vine-ceilinged "grotto" provide two alfresco options (one sunny, one shady). Out here you'll also find one of the residents' favourite features: an outdoor shower. The smart shower screen was commissioned by Merano designer Harry Thaler and crafted onsite by weaving damp willow branches around a metal frame.

It's on the second – and busiest – floor, though, where this mix of South Tyrolean handiwork and the residents' international taste blurs best. A balcony opens up to a sunroom sporting modernist furniture by Josef Frank and a side table by US

designer TH Robsjohn-Gibbings. There's Japanese woodblock art aplenty but the focal point is a magnificent illustrated world map drawn in Sweden, circa 1935. A clever built-in drinks cabinet – made from oak, marble and cast metal – resides here too and opens to reveal an Aladdin's cave of alcohol.

Despite local help, this is a residence reflective of its owners; a house with finds from a life's worth of travelling. From a "Made in Melbourne" Angelucci sofa to a vintage Bell Canada telephone and a hand-drawn sketch from Oscar Niemeyer to Murano glass lamps secured at a nearby second-hand shop, a world of good design has its place here. But there are additions from closer to home too. "Our aim was to keep it roughly within the old Austrian empire, either Swiss, Austrian, German or Italian," says one of the residents. "I think we have come pretty good on that."

1. The neighbouring snow-capped Dolomites 2. Italian-made loungers waiting for the residents to soak up the sun 3. Builders matched the new oak fittings with the original timber fixtures; print by Stefan Oláh 4. Plants line the light-filled stairway where the 1960s handrail curves elegantly upwards

2   3

4

1. A leafy view surrounds the living room where a Florence Knoll sofa, lounge chairs and two benches create a sociable space 2. Illustrations by Jordi Labanda overlooking modernist furniture and vintage Scandinavian pieces

1   2

1

2

3   4

5   6

7   8

1. An angular entranceway 2. Chevron artwork by Virge 3. Table by Switzerland's USM; the chair came with the house 4. Glassware dresses
up the windowsill 5. Vintage Lotte lamps and a colourful painting, also by Virge, in the master bedroom 6. Egg yolk tiles in the upstairs bathroom
7. A morning newspaper read on Swiss outdoor café furniture by Manufakt 8. Italian glasses from Stillsegler

1

1. In the living room, a 1940s Svenskt Tenn 311 sofa and stools surround a low coffee table, where plenty of hardbacks give the finishing touches
2. Natural light illuminates the kitchen

Ceramic artist Karin Widnäs has created a space almost entirely from indigenous wood and handmade tiles.

3

The handcrafted home
Fiskars, Finland

1

Architect:
Tuomo Siitonen

Year built:
2005

Size:
350 sq m

Key materials:
Wood sourced from
the local forest.

**What makes it
unique:** The house
is filled with the
owner's handmade
ceramics, from the
tiles on the walls and
floors to artworks.

**The owner's
favourite element:**
"My home and studio
are surrounded by
nature with a huge
forest on one side and
a beautiful lake on
the other. What more
could you wish for?"

In a coniferous forest on the shores of
Lake Degersjö in Finland, a large wooden
house sits on a ridge overlooking the
water. It is the home and studio of Finnish
ceramic artist Karin Widnäs. "I knew
already in the 1980s that I wanted to use
ceramics in building and I decided to
do everything myself," she says, exuding
the same air of serenity that envelops her
home. "The tiles on the floors, the walls,
the sinks and fireplace – I made them all
to show that it can be done."

The building itself, which was designed
by Helsinki-based architect Tuomo Siitonen
and took 10 years to complete, consists
of two distinct spaces that share the same
copper-clad roof but are divided by an
external covered corridor. Widnäs works in
the first and lives in the second. "Making
ceramics is messy. When I leave my studio,
I enter another realm – my home," she says.

The structure is made almost entirely
from indigenous wood cut by local craftsmen:
the beams and the planks are spruce, the
terrace floor is larch while the exterior is
clad in untreated wood. But rather than
retreating into nature, the result here is
a colour that changes as the house ages –
the light shade of the fresh wood is now a
silver hue. "I love this colour. In the evening
sun, its glow reminds me of the countryside
barns of my youth," Widnäs says.

Inside, waxed spruce flooring in the
living room blends seamlessly into the
wooden pillars and the sloped ceiling.

2

1. The building's exterior is clad in untreated wood 2. Nikari oak chairs line the table; artwork by Karin Widnäs is displayed at the end of the room

1. The glass-lined living room looks out onto the surrounding forest and lake

1

1

A wall of glass that faces the lake merges the boundary between interior and exterior where a tall ageing pine tree seems as though it is trying to reach inside and touch the white Ligne Roset armchair by the fireplace. "To sit here and see the treetops dance in the wind against the turquoise sky... Who needs a TV?" she says.

In fact, there is hardly a single electrical appliance in the house: no stereo, television or any kitchen equipment (other than a microwave). This same austerity extends to the turf-roofed sauna outside, which stands a metre off the ground and has no electric lights or running water. The smell of ageing aspen and the moist moss of the Finnish forest bed fills the air. To Widnäs, the sauna, much like the rest of her home, is a source of inspiration and creativity: "It breathes and connects us with nature."

Most of the art in the house consists of ceramic works by Widnäs and her friends but there are a few exceptions: a lounge chair next to the bed was made from willow by the late Fiskars artist Markku Kosonen and a piece entitled "Curly" by Finnish-American sculptor Howard Smith – another local – resides in the living room.

Throughout the house, there is a palpable sense of cosiness. It is the home of someone who has spent an entire life working with natural materials and tangible objects. "When I moved here in 1995, I was considered crazy but I liked how it made me feel. It still gives me immense energy."

2

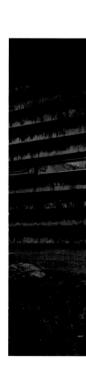

3

1. Widnäs made all the tiles in the house 2. Widnäs cosies up by the fire on a Ligne Roset armchair 3. Sleeping under timber ceilings 4. The home glows like a lantern 5. Handmade tiles provide a colourful backdrop for some greenery

4

5

This playful restoration of an old mariner's cottage expertly walks the line between experimentation and respect for heritage, while making the most of its world-class views.

4
The farmhouse conversion
Tasmania, Australia

1. Wardle's waterfront farm is shared with his 2,000-strong flock of sheep 2. The living room window seat is a suntrap

Just off the coast of Tasmania lies Bruny Island, a small outcrop of land populated by only 600 people. It is here that Melbourne architect John Wardle and his wife bought a waterfront farm – now home to a sizeable flock of sheep – in 2002. On their first visit, the pair made a beeline for the coast and marvelled at the view. Only after they had turned around did they appreciate the small house near the cliff edge. It was built by the farm's first owner Captain James Kelly in the 1840s.

For several years, Wardle dreamed of restoring the cottage. He knew it would be time-consuming so, in the meantime, he decided to build a small structure – the Shearer's Quarters – where guests and staff could stay. But he never lost sight of his ambition for Captain Kelly's Cottage. "Part of it was a sense of responsibility: I had a curious desire to make more of it."

It wasn't until February 2017 that the cottage was completed, after 18 months of work. Wardle's first step was to remove the misjudged alterations by past owners: a series of clumsy extensions linking the house's two oldest sections were replaced with an enclosed living area where multi-paned windows allow light to filter in.

Architect:
The cottage was restored in 2017 by owner John Wardle. He built the Shearers Quarters in 2011.

Year built:
1840s

Size:
The cottage is 180 sq m; the Shearer's Quarters is 136 sq m.

Key materials:
Original brickwork and Tasmanian eucalyptus.

What makes it unique:
Its sympathetic yet playful renovation.

The owner's favourite element:
"The living room with its retractable timber windows and screens, linear daybeds and view out is a sublime place for contemplation."

1

2

1. All surfaces and elements are made with Tasmanian timber 2. Multi-paned windows flood the space with light 3. A gabled ceiling was created for the historic kitchen 4. Shutters retract to open up the house 5. Custom-designed shelving 6. An axe handle takes the place of a door handle

2

3

4

5 6

1

1. Floor-to-ceiling windows open up to reveal the surrounding landscape 2. The original verandah was completely rebuilt

1. The new living area takes advantage of its location, looking both north and south into separate coves; the room is furnished with comfortable Patricia Urquiola-designed chairs

Wardle lined the walls, floor and ceiling with Tasmanian oak while retractable shutters were added to the outer walls to provide a shield against inclement weather.

In the kitchen, the building's history becomes the focus. Original brick walls remain exposed, save for a few custom-built shelves. Japanese tiles frame an Aga oven and a rectangular alcove holds firewood. Over some of the doors, the words "Mind your head" gleam in gold letters, a light-hearted warning directed at Wardle's tall son. It's one of many playful design elements; at the rear of the cottage Wardle has erected an antique bell in tribute to Captain Kelly. On the main entrance, he's swapped doorknobs for axe handles. "There's something about the building's story that is best said with a degree of humour," he says. "I didn't want the house to feel constrained with the seriousness of heritage restoration."

For Wardle, seeing his family discover the full extent of the cottage's charm comes with a deep sense of satisfaction. "There were times when I speculated whether it would be a success. Now it feels like it was worth taking the risk all those years ago."

1

*Saved from demolition in the 1950s, this grand Georgian abode is
a tribute to its owner and a lifetime dedicated to the modernist aesthetic.*

5
The terraced townhouse
Bristol, UK

1

Year built:
Originally constructed
in the 1820s, it was
restored in the 1960s.

Size:
The house comprises
five generous floors.

Key materials:
Stucco façade on brick.

What makes it unique:
Its original features,
which were saved from
modernisation when it
fell into disrepair.

**The owner's
favourite element:**
"The hillside position."

2

3

"I was 16 when I bought my first pot,"
recalls Ken Stradling from his living
room overlooking Bristol's River Avon.
"It was a piece of Elton Ware from
Clevedon [in Somerset, UK]. They were
pulling down a Georgian house and
the contents were being sold at auction."

His own elegant five-storey townhouse
narrowly missed the same fate. It was
destined for the wrecking ball before he
and his wife, artist Betty Haggar, bought
it for £100 in 1958. The council told them
the house was in such disrepair that it
wouldn't last 15 years. "The whole area
was down for demolition," says Stradling.

The pair faced a daunting task: the
first-floor wrought iron balcony had
crashed into the garden below; debris
was piled knee-high inside and the house
lacked basic amenities like electricity
and modern plumbing. Despite the local
council having rejected their application
for a restoration grant (the letter for which
now hangs proudly above the toilet), they
got to work preserving the home's period
features, fireplaces and cornices.

Today, every surface in the south-
facing terrace is covered with Stradling's
vast collection of glass, pots and plates.

1. A rosewood dining chair by Niels Møller 2. Stradling's art collection lines the walls 3. Pinned-up postcards 4. A shelf in the study 5. The house is in Bristol's Hotwells area 6. A collection of 1950s Poole pottery sits on the mantelpiece above a Danish cherrywood desk in the study

4

5

6

1. The light-filled first-floor sitting room is home to Stradling's glass collection, which includes pieces by Venini, Orrefors and Holmegaard

They were amassed on his buying trips to Denmark, Sweden, Finland and Italy – as well as at UK auction houses – while at the helm of the Bristol Guild of Applied Art shop. "You'll find a piece worth £4,000 next to something worth £5," he says while handling a tea service by Walter Gropius for German company Rosenthal.

For decades, Stradling travelled Europe bringing back furniture, design and craft to sell to a UK audience. He admits that during these foreign forays he nearly always acquired something for himself – and such pieces are clearly visible in his home. In the living space, Bauhaus side-tables, Scandinavian glass and Somerset ceramics live side by side. A private sitting room is home to an early Gordon Russell oak side table, English studio pottery, wooden figures by Sam Smith and a 1960s rosewood chair by Niels Møller. Feet away, a bright orange Murano glass vase sits on a 19th-century Indian provincial wooden chest.

But while Stradling's double-fronted rooms showcase a tour de force of mid-century design, this is no museum. From thick Afghan carpets to the 1970s-era BeoGram 1500 record player and the well-stocked bookshelves, the space is intimate, warm and friendly. He is passionate that design should be touched, handled (despite the risk of priceless breakages) and better understood. "I have had so much fun looking at these things," he says.

Designed by maverick architect Rudolph Michael Schindler, this light-filled home in California has been brought back to its former glory.

6
The restored masterpiece
Los Angeles, USA

For Noel Osheroff, an artist born in 1929, home is a hilltop property overlooking the Silver Lake Reservoir in Los Angeles. It's the same house her parents brought her to in 1934 and it's where she returned after six decades to restore the space that shaped her – one of the finest ever designed by the maverick California modernist Rudolph Michael Schindler.

While 60 years had passed since Osheroff (née Oliver) last occupied her family's residence, little had changed. The cubist volumes still cantilevered over the street, the curved handrail still swept upwards from the kerb to the front door and the wing-like roof still hovered overhead, with walls of glass on every side.

Architect:
Rudolph Michael Schindler

Year built:
1933

Size:
148 sq m

Key materials:
Glass, wood and stucco.

What makes it unique: The house was a harbinger of things to come – pioneering glass walls were custom built while Schindler made the most of the pitched roof with soaring ceilings.

The owner's favourite element:
"The way it makes me feel. Thanks to the glass-filled walls, the house is bathed in light from sunrise to sunset with a view of the beautiful greenery outside. It feels like you are out in nature even though you are in the middle of the city."

1   2

1. Vast windows look out over the Silver Lake Reservoir 2. Californian sunshine lights up timber furnishings 3. Noel Osheroff

1

2

3

1. Doorway to the terrace 2. The restored stucco exteriors 3. A sculpture by Osheroff's mother, Stephanie Oliver 4. Objects from Osheroff's collection
5. Built-in sofa 6. Plywood chair in the style of Schindler, made by Osheroff's son 7. The wing-like roof seems to float above the glass partitions

1. The cantilevered roof offers some much-needed shade to an outdoor dining area

1

1

Even the sculptural plywood shelves still projected from the built-in sofa in the living room.

Schindler was particularly proud of the Oliver House, singling it out as a "revolutionary design" that "blends harmoniously with both the hill and the sky". His clients felt the same. Bill Oliver, a folk-singing journalist, encountered Schindler when covering a performance at the architect's pioneering 1922 Hollywood home. Dazzled by its flat roof, communal plan, openness to the outdoors and materials palette, he informed Stephanie, his sculptor wife, that he'd "met the man who will build our house". And that house became the place where the Olivers lived out the rest of their days.

"If anything should happen to me," Stephanie would tell her daughter, "hang on to the house!" Osheroff obeyed. Yet as Schindler's posthumous reputation grew, the Oliver House languished with decades of tenants obscuring key elements and neglecting others.

Surveying the newly restored living room Osheroff reflects on what drew her back. "This house was never really finished," she says. "My parents didn't

have any money; they got just far enough to move in. All my life I kept thinking, 'Someone should shape this house up.'"

That someone ended up being Osheroff. Sub-contractors were hired to replace the systems; her sons helped out as well but much of the work she did herself. She sanded layers of dark stain from Schindler's signature plywood cabinets and reapplied the tint she recalled from childhood; she resurrected the original tan of the stucco and the golden rod of the trim. The vast windows were rehung; even the architect's bespoke dining benches, lost to history, were recreated. Osheroff even tamed years of overgrown garden and helped refresh the bathrooms and kitchen.

The Oliver House was finally "finished" in 2018. It continues to convey, as Schindler put it, "a startling effect of space, light, cleanliness [and] simplicity", with patterns of sun and shade permeating its glass partitions and playing across its bare walls. "It really is a rare thing: a very good example of a simple little house," says Osheroff. "It's direct, even cheap. And I want it to remain here, like this, as a testament to that idea."

2

1. Verdant views from the bedroom 2. A glimpse of the office 3. Osheroff recreated the bespoke dining furniture 4. Bird ornaments

3

4

With a structure that frames the surrounding landscape in spectacular widescreen, this pared-back residence is a masterclass in modesty.

7
The island escape
Mallorca, Spain

If you tried to mark the epicentre of Mallorca on a map, it's likely your inky cross would land where this stripped-to-its-essence house has been built. This isn't the landscape that people usually think of when the island is mentioned: there are no beaches in sight; the Mediterranean is off stage. Instead there is a long view of stony wheat fields, almond trees and *fincas*, all rolling away to the mountainous horizon.

It's this landscape that informed the home, designed by Jaime Oliver and Paloma Hernaiz of Palma architecture firm Ohlab. The client wanted to make a house that would come in on a budget and take much of its richness from the view. "The exercise of taking scissors to a project leaves you with what is important," says Oliver.

A modest property, this single-storey home is just six metres wide and 31 metres long, bookended by bedrooms. The key space sits in the middle: a living area with doors that slide away, front and back, to allow air to charge through. This opens up to become as one with the terraces on both sides of the house. Adding continuity to this indoors-outdoors arena is the pinky concrete slab that extends throughout and the cane roof, which starts on the outdoor

Architects:
Jaime Oliver and
Paloma Hernaiz

Year built:
2019

Size:
186 sq m

Key materials:
Concrete, tiles, cane
and lime mortars.

**What makes it
unique:** Its traditional
architecture with a
focus on sustainability
and energy efficiency.

**The owner's
favourite element:**
"The north terrace –
there are incredible
panoramic views of the
countryside from here.
In the summer months,
the living room opens
onto this space which
then connects directly
with the land; the
whole house feels at
one with nature and
the surroundings."

1

1. The living space features a Valldemossa sofa by Borek covered with antique kilim, rocking chair and Robusta lounge chair with matching footstool from local brand La Pecera; the seating area is lit by the Nuvol Double floorlamp by Contain while the dining table is illuminated by a Santa & Cole pendant

1

2

3

canopy, runs across the lounge and beyond. The shaded areas and through-air help to make this a house where there is no need for air-con – even in the summer. Sustainability is key to their thinking.

To frame the incredible view, the duo built the front opening with a cinematic flair. "With the doors slid back, the opening is the same ratio as the screens that we had in cinemas when we were kids; when you are in the house you are sort of making a movie of your life," says Oliver.

Modest materials were used to keep costs in check: tiles were left over from another project, concrete sinks were found on sale at local firm Huguet while the roof supports are similar to those used to erect agricultural buildings. But they couldn't – and didn't want to – avoid some costs. The planning consent made clear this would have to be a home that reflected the area's vernacular architecture. Colours were prescribed, shutters attached to windows and the roof was set out to the centimetre.

The building may be small, quiet and restrained but as the light fades, all feels good in the world. This is a simple home that proves humble materials, a little creativity and a good view can create something truly magnificent.In this tucked-away spot, the landscape has joined forces with Ohlab to make you think about what's really important.

4

5

1. The bedroom 2. Terrace with a pair of mid-century bamboo loungers 3. View of the kitchen, with wall tiles from Huguet; the bar stool and dining chairs are also from La Pecera 4. The barrelling countryside 5. Kitchen with concrete roof supports

An oft-overlooked pioneer of mid-century modernism, Mario Pani's meticulously designed Mexican residences are much coveted.

8
The art-filled apartment
Mexico City, Mexico

Architect and urbanist Mario Pani was Mexico's answer to Le Corbusier: a mid-century renaissance man, he experimented with urban models from clever apartment buildings for the upwardly mobile to huge housing projects. One of the finest examples of his work can be found in the capital's Cuauhtémoc district – a residential block built between 1943 and 1945 in red-brick and glass. It's here that Yolanda Jimenez has made her home.

Jimenez is what you might call a Pani mega-fan; "I'd wanted to live in this building for years," she says. On entering the apartment, the first things to catch the eye are the unusually high ceilings and a set of curved windows that allow light to filter in through the trees. From the front door, stairs lead up to an ample living room dominated by a creamy-pink sofa and Moroccan rug containing shocks of pink, yellow and brown.

A set of steps leads from the living room – where an original piece by German-Mexican artist Mathias Goeritz (a frequent Pani collaborator) hangs on the wall – to a floor that's been cut away to allow the room below to reach impressive heights. Here you'll find more intimate areas including a dining room, guest bedroom and what Jimenez refers to as the library. Packed with objects such as Mayan ceramics and antique masks, there are also chairs by Don Shoemaker, a Nebraskan who moved to Mexico and crafted modernist pieces in dark wood. It's in this room that Jimenez gets to appreciate her "favourite thing by Pani": the curving shape of the building's brickwork exterior, viewable to the side of a balcony that's filled with large cacti.

Pani's sites are particularly popular with those in the creative industries, including gallerists, photographers, artists and architects – or in Jimenez's case, the owner of a mezcal brand. When asked, most state similar reasons for this: in an ever-denser metropolis, it's almost impossible to find buildings with the same generosity of space and attention to detail. "Pani thought about the moments you spend in a place and your mindset," says Jimenez. "I don't think architecture is like that anymore."

Pani often designed with a technique that he called *dos en tres* (two in three), which meant laying out two apartments over three floors and playing with room dimensions to create different moods in each. For Jimenez, it's a wonder that Pani never received the same global recognition as compatriots such as Luis Barragán and Pedro Ramírez Vázquez. "Barragán's personality tells you where to look. But Pani was open; you feel relaxed. I have light and space in every room, every corner. It makes it hard to leave the house."

Architect
Mario Pani

Year built
1943 to 1945

Size
260 sq m

Key materials
Red brick and glass.

What makes it unique: It is one of Mario Pani's most iconic Mexico City buildings – its pioneering structural system allowed it to tower above other residential blocks of its time.

The owner's favourite element:
"The apartment is divided into three-storeys, which gives every room a different feeling. You move from a narrow hallway onto a bright living room with a five-metre-high ceiling – instead of feeling controlled by the journey you are invited from one room to the other. I rediscover the light every morning."

1

1. Floor-to-ceiling windows look out onto a leafy view 2. Chairs by Don Shoemaker in the library provide the perfect viewpoint of the building's brickwork
3. A painting found at a nearby flea market hangs above the greenery-filled fireplace 4. The exterior of Pani's 1940s Cuauhtémoc apartment building

2

3 4

1

1. Stairs lead up to the mezzanine level 2. In the living room, a circular coffee table by Greta Grossman – one of Jimenez's favourite pieces in the apartment – reflects the curved shape of the windows behind

1. A dining table and chairs by Pierre Jeanneret adorn an airy corner 2. Mayan ceramics and antique masks decorate the walls of the library while a Serge Mouille light illuminates a cosy reading spot 3. Woven side tables sit alongside a daybed by Frank Kyle on the mezzanine level

2

3

This unassuming cottage – which is essentially a series of interconnecting wooden boxes – is a window into Cape Cod's creative past.

9
The coastal summer house
Cape Cod, USA

In 1960, Robert Hatch – a film critic and editor at *The Nation* magazine – and his artist wife Ruth commissioned self-taught designer Jack Hall to create a summer house on Cape Cod, the tendril of land that stretches out from the Massachusetts mainland into the Atlantic Ocean. Hall completed the single-storey building two years later and, despite having no formal training in architecture, it was added to the USA's register of historic places in 2014. Perched atop a windswept bluff in Wellfleet overlooking Cape Cod Bay, the house was a radical experiment in how modernist design principles could be applied to the area's vernacular of wood-constructed homes.

"Hall loved the old buildings, but he also loved modernism – Japanese metabolism, modularity and prefabrication," says Peter McMahon, a designer and the founder of the Cape Cod Modern House Trust, a conservancy that restored the cottage in 2013. "He would mash the design styles together in ways that are quite successful."

The Hatches were part of a vibrant intellectual community on Cape Cod, which included Bauhaus founder Walter Gropius, Finnish modernist Eero Saarinen and designer Marcel Breuer – all of whom built their own summer homes to modernist principles scattered around the area's wooded and pond-pocked landscape.

"When I first came upon Hatch Cottage years ago," McMahon says, "I couldn't figure out what it was. It was such a mysterious object." Central to Hall's design – which appears deceptively simple – is this sense of mystery. Held together by slender wooden frames, the house comprises a series of wooden boxes, which are connected by outdoor "corridors", meaning you have to go outside to move from one to the other.

"The building is brilliantly sited – the winter wind blows over it because it's nestled down in the brow of the hill with a spectacular view of the bay," McMahon adds. "It appears as if it is floating; it hovers above the land in this surreal way."

1

1. A wood-burning stove creates a warm and cosy atmosphere in the dining area where design classics such as Alvar Aalto stools and antique Hitchcock chairs sit beside simple built-in furniture and artwork painted by Ruth Hatch

1

Architect
Jack Hall

Year built
1962

Size
73 sq m

Key materials
Douglas fir from the
Pacific Northwest.

**What makes it
unique:** Its layout –
outdoor pathways
connect the rooms,
which are in effect
wooden boxes.

**Peter McMahon's
favourite element:**
"The many large and
small shutters, which
open and shut to
regulate fresh air, light
and views out onto
the bay. In warm
weather the house
is porous but when
closed up in winter it
becomes a mysterious
solid object."

Hall melded the boundaries between
indoors and out elsewhere too. The
rooms' outer-facing walls, clad in panels
of vertical fir siding, can be opened
upwards with pulleys allowing daylight
– and breathtaking views – to stream
in. While open, the panels serve as
awnings that create squares of shade
on the property's outer walkway.

If Hall followed few conventions in
the design of the cottage, the same could
be said for the Hatches' furnishing of it:
original stools by Alvar Aalto sit alongside
antique Hitchcock chairs, seashells
collected from the beach below and many
paintings by Ruth herself. "It's an eclectic
mix," McMahon says, "much like the
building. It is hyper-modern but it also
looks like an old piece of driftwood."

Originally created as an antidote to
the stresses of 1960s urban living, today
Hatch Cottage serves as a holiday house
for appreciators of modernist design
and a place of pilgrimage for nearby
architecture students. And it's hard to
imagine a more relaxing or inspiring
setting: the sheer natural beauty of Cape
Cod with its ponds, woods and sand dunes
compliments the cottage perfectly.

2

3

1. Rice paper pendant lights illuminate the rustic wood-panelled interior 2. Open shelves display personal items and utensils in the kitchen
3. Hatch Cottage looks out over Cape Cod Bay

This elegant late-19th-century Swedish apartment houses a collection of finds gathered by a couple with distinctive taste.

10

The eclectic abode

Stockholm, Sweden

The entrance to Emma Ohlson's building is grand, even for this part of Stockholm, which has no shortage of stately structures. The lofty dimensions are due to the fact that in the late 1800s it was designed to receive horse-drawn carriages en route to the courtyard stables. "I fell in love with the entrance," says Ohlson, who has lived in the third-floor apartment with her husband Andreas and their children since 2014. "I immediately thought: this is what I want to come home to."

An interest in design and interiors has always been a part of Ohlson's life; it's a passion that has grown stronger as she and her husband have renovated homes. "We both really enjoy creating indoor spaces that feel just right and we're learning from our mistakes along the way."

The focal point of the apartment's living space is the ornate octagonal dining room. Ohlson likes to work there during the week when her children are at school. She explains that eating and entertaining are central to the home, with large dinners held at the large round Danish Svend Dyrlund table, which is softly lit by a Hans Agne Jakobsson chandelier. This is just one of the many beautiful light fixtures around the property: there are lamps by Scolari, Lumina and other pieces picked up at auctions and flea markets.

From the dining area, lit by brass lamps, rooms unfurl like the folds of a fan.

2

Architect:
Carl Möller

Year built:
1883

Size:
200 sq m

Key materials:
Inside, original pine floorboards are laid throughout with paned limestone in the hallways and kitchen.

What makes it unique: Its grand entranceway.

The apartment opens onto an unusual octagonal dining room, complete with an original tiled fireplace.

The owner's favourite element:
"The kitchen. Even though it's not very big it is very functional and serves as the perfect gathering point for friends and family with a table for dinners and a bar for pre and after-dinner drinks."

1

3

1. Cosmo the labrador takes a break 2. Ohlson's collections top a smart console table 3. Vintage armchairs from the Decorative Antiques & Textiles Fair in Battersea, London, beneath an artwork by Katarina Rundqvist in the library

1. In the living room, a leather sofa that once belonged to Ohlson's grandfather and two aluminium armchairs by Mats Theselius are placed around an Eames Elliptical table. Behind, a tapestry by Pasi Wälimaa hangs above a mid-century sideboard

1

1

1. A Hans Agne Jakobsson chandelier illuminates the hallway-cum-dining space 2. An Enzo Mari daybed sits opposite one of the two original fireplaces

The high ceilings give poise to the rooms, while the old, slightly imperfect glass in the windows creates a dreamy lustre – augmented by softly coloured walls. "Many think that white has always been the colour used on joinery but we've painted borders and double doors grey – a similar shade was commonly used on wood in Swedish homes in the 1800s," Ohlson says.

In the living room, the centrepiece is a leather sofa inherited from Ohlson's grandfather. Opposite an original Eames Elliptical table (sometimes known as the "surfboard table") are two round-backed aluminium armchairs by Swedish designer Mats Theselius. "They were a find but one of the chairs had a small dent," she says. "It was made worse when I thought I was strong enough to carry it – and dropped it." In the tranquil library, two low-slung leather armchairs (the first items the couple bought together) sit beneath a painting by Andreas's sister Katarina Rundqvist, which adds a touch of pink to the otherwise understated room. "We have a 'his' and 'hers'. They're incredibly comfortable and so us."

The living room and dining area both feature majestic tiled fireplaces; there used to be one in each room but the others were removed once modern heating was installed. And when the long Swedish winter nights draw in, these fireplaces become central to the home: "as the dark months come around, most Stockholmers stay indoors," Ohlson says. "Perhaps that's why we spend so much time and money on our homes – to feel snug and cosy when we have to hide away until spring."

1

1. A vintage chandelier casts a warming glow in the kitchen 2. A collection of *objets* displayed on the windowsill, which is painted in a shade of grey similar to one used in the 1800s 3. Textiles and pattern in the master bedroom 4. The grand foyer of the building 5. Emma Ohlson takes in the view

2

3

4

5

Crafting an idyllic retreat within the confines of a city as chaotic as Jakarta is no mean feat, but this home manages to preserve its stunning natural setting.

11
The urban oasis
Jakarta, Indonesia

1

When Ronald Akili decided that it was time to find a better quality of life for his family, he didn't just start on his own home. The entrepreneur, co-founder of hospitality brand Potato Head, discovered a site in south Jakarta and worked with Indonesian architect Andra Matin to design 20 houses, one of which was to be his. "The spot was perfect," adds Akili. "The contours of the land were interesting and the plant growth was lush."

The family moved into the house – which feels a world away from Jakarta's urban chaos – in 2011. An inner-city oasis, this verdant, quiet structure opens onto a wood-decked courtyard at the heart of the home. "We designed the house by looking at how we want to run our life," says Akili. "We want the kids to be exposed to being outdoors. Lots of kids grow up surrounded by a concrete jungle, glued to screens. We want to be outside of that hectic lifestyle."

Architect: Andra Matin

Year built: 2011

Size: 900 sq m

Key materials: Local wood and concrete.

What makes it unique: Its sustainable approach: mature trees have been built into the home while the nearby lake is used as a water recycling centre.

The owner's favourite element: "The kitchen – it opens onto the courtyard for alfresco dining on one side and overlooks the lush vegetable garden on the other."

2

1. The house was designed to fit into its natural surroundings 2. The wood-decked courtyard is the heart of the home

1. Each room has a specific function; the living room is for reading

1. Floor-to-ceiling windows blur divisions between inside and out 2. Personal artwork abounds 3. Plants grow in, on and around the house
4. The building's exterior 5. Mid-century furniture and wood panelling add warmth to the master bedroom 6. Textured geometric tiles on the façade

1

2

3

5

4

6

1

To foster this environment, Akili and
Matin designed a house where every room,
apart from the courtyard, has a specific
function. "There's no large indoor space
where people can hang out," says Akili.
"If we want to cook or eat, we head to
the kitchen. If we want to read, the living
room. There's only one television, which
is in the kids' playroom. This means the
courtyard is the main communal area."

Sliding glass doors open on both sides
of the property allowing the kitchen and
dining space to become as one with the
inner courtyard and the surrounding
landscape, including the fields and the
nearby lake of Tanah Teduh, where Akili
and his sons like to go fishing. Stairs to the
four bedrooms on the second floor set off
from the courtyard, while the living room
leads onto a separate well-planted terrace –
there is greenery everywhere you look.

Despite its contemporary appearance,
Akili was keen to keep a classic feel to
the house. "Old-fashioned living is what
I perceive as good quality of life," he
says. "We get to breathe fresh air here.
The kids have plenty of activities. This
is our sanctuary and we want to keep it
as traditional as possible."

2   3

1. A set of MR chairs by Mies van der Rohe for Knoll surround a table in the open-plan kitchen and dining space 2. In the central courtyard furniture is set among tropical foliage 3. The well-planted vegetable garden

A disused site in central Madrid has been transformed into a space where a husband-and-wife team can both live and work with all the creature comforts.

12
The home and studio
Madrid, Spain

1

"Downsizing doesn't always have to be a compromise," says David Iglesias Resina. "In our case, smaller has meant better," adds his wife, Mexican-born architect Melina Carranza Maciel. The couple moved into this long-abandoned space in Madrid in 2013, following a mutual decision to start afresh. They have been busy building their small leather-goods brand, Oficio Studio, and furnishing a comfortable home here ever since.

Tucked away behind the museums and galleries of Paseo del Prado, the three-storey building was originally built in the 1860s for a large Spanish family and was eventually divided into separate residences. Previously a sculptor's and then a painter's studio, the long open-plan space had endured more than a decade of disrepair by the time the pair discovered it. Attracted by the high ceilings and sun-drenched terrace, they saw it as an opportunity for both refuge and relief.

Once in, the pair focused on creating a space that was conducive to both comfort and creativity. The transition as far from smooth. "We had to install a kitchen and repair the ceiling just to make it habitable," says Iglesias Resina.

2

3

1. Wooden floorboards meet timber-panelled walls 2. Art-filled workstation 3. Iglesias Resina and Carranza Maciel made the coffee table, light fixtures, sofa and cushions that fill the living quarters

1. Sun-drenched terrace 2. Airy wooden-beamed bedroom

1

1. Carranza Maciel and Iglesias Resina with their dog Pedales 2. Handcrafted axe-cover made by Iglesias

Architect:
The three-storey building was built for a large Spanish family.

Year built:
1860

Size:
140 sq m

Key materials:
Inside the brick building, industrial components sit beside leather swatches and plentiful greenery.

What makes it unique: Its multi-use space – the owners transformed it into an open-plan area perfect for working and living.

The owners' favourite element:
"The terrace. It is here that we like to watch sunsets and dine among the fragrant jasmine bushes."

The pair's handiwork can be seen throughout: they restored old relics of furniture and designed original pieces and fittings. The coffee table, light fixtures and sofa were all welded together by the couple; the cushions were cut, filled and sewn with the antique sewing machines that line the wall of their workshop.

A few metres from their neatly organised workspace sits a kitchen and living area, coloured by the multi-hued spines of books – pointedly there is no television. A prominent collection of potted plants adds colour to the wooden furnishings and tempers the industrial machinery that dominates the other half of their quarters. It is clear that the couple's combined workspace and home is not just an expression of their desire for a slower pace, it also catalogues the gentle evolution of their mindset since moving here.

They are adamant that striking the right work-life balance has become easier because it is no longer complicated by a time-consuming commute. Carranza Maciel believes that building comfort into the daily grind has also spurred their creativity. "Why would we want to over complicate things?" she says with a smile.

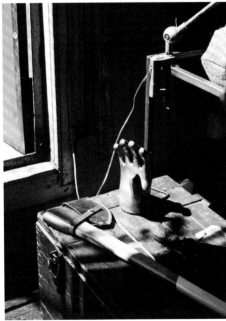

1

2

1. The glass-lined home is set among eucalyptus, pine and cork trees 2. Sliding glass doors open the spacious living room up to the elements 3. Pots and pans are within easy reach 4. Shelves are dotted with crockery 5. Local logs are used to heat the lodge

Going off-grid presents benefits and challenges and this clever project exemplifies the pros and mitigates the cons in a charming and cosy manner.

13
The self-sufficient retreat
Alentejo, Portugal

Having grown up in Calabria – a wild and beautiful southern Italian region bordered by both the Tyrrhenian and Ionian seas – hospitality entrepreneur and designer Francesco Ippolito has always appreciated living in close contact with nature. Which is exactly what drew him to Comporta in Portugal, an unspoilt coastal region with a year-round temperate climate. "When you wish to muster new energy and nourish your mind and body, there is no better place than Alentejo's coast," says Ippolito. It is here that he decided to build himself an off-the-grid home in the vast countryside. "I immediately felt as though I was widening my horizons."

Completed in 2015, the home is part of Monte da Gala Eco Resort – a high-end, sustainable hospitality development – and sits on the lush site amid eucalyptus, pine and cork trees. Ippolito took inspiration from Philip Johnson's Glass House and Mies van der Rohe's Farnsworth House, creating a simple building of glass volumes and generous dimensions. Timber fixtures that will age gracefully lend warmth to the structure.

While off-the-grid living might mean sacrificing a few luxuries – a novel outdoor shower Ippolito co-designed to reuse rainwater being a case in point – nature still provides many creature comforts here. Ample sunlight streams in and allows the home to feel bright and inviting during the day, while future plans to install solar panels will see the property powered by the sun's energy.

Inside, the interiors reflect Ippolito's sustainable, self-sufficient ethos: aside from simple, built-in furniture, everything else in the home was made, found or repurposed. Throughout, glass bottles hang from the ceiling as pendant lights while the material that clads the interior has been used to create a lampshade that diffuses soft light above the dining table. Elsewhere, a rustic coffee table and headboard have been crafted from wooden pallets and the steel seen on the roof lines the walls of an indoor shower. The effect is bucolic bliss.

"My interiors are essential and minimal, the space has to be neutral and let the nature around you play the main role," he says.

Ippolito is keen to share his vision and appreciation of sustainable living with others. In fact, for Ippolito, the home's modularity is its most important feature: the design can be easily duplicated, meaning that future suites on this site will be quick to construct and affordable to build. "Our objective is to attract customers who appreciate contemporary design more than the redundant decoration of, say, a grand hotel," Ippolito says of the development. "The focus is the full immersion in nature."

4 5

Architect:
The homeowner, Francesco Ippolito

Year built:
2015

Size:
124 sq m

Key materials:
Wood, corten steel and glass.

What makes it unique: Its self-sufficient and sustainable design.

The owner's favourite element:
"The direct and unfiltered contact with the surrounding landscape. I can literally say I live in the middle of nature."

1

1. In the living room, the furniture was either built-in, handmade or found and restored 2. Interior walls are made from sustainable and local materials
3. A feline friend 4. The master bedroom has unobstructed views of nature

2

3

4

Living in the former home of an architect is a privilege – but it also comes with responsibility. The occupants of Børge Mogensen's house got the balance just right.

14
The design classic
Gentofte, Denmark

1

Monika and Ole Paustian promised each other one thing when they bought the home of their friend Børge Mogensen, the revered Danish architect who died in 1972: they would not live in a tomb. The couple, founders of design retailer Paustian, moved into the property in the municipality of Gentofte, north of Copenhagen, in 2012.

Set between a bog and dense woods, the house was built in 1957 by architect Erling Zeuthen Nielsen in collaboration with Mogensen. It was not just the latter's home but his self-proclaimed "laboratory". It is here that he drew up plans for his iconic furniture, making prototypes to test for everyday use – with a little help from his children's playmates, obligingly spilling drinks on the leather upholstery – some of which still fill the house.

When the designer's widow Alice passed away, architects and museums demanded that the house be preserved. Since moving in, the Paustians have treated the place with respect – not just for its place in design history but for Mogensen's original intention: for the house to be a home. "I like his sense of style but to me he can be a bit square and practical," says German-born Monika. "So we replaced and added a few things."

Despite these adjustments, the house remains firmly in Mogensen's spirit – it had been lovingly maintained by Alice before the Paustians bought it.

Architect:
Erling Zeuthen Nielsen in collaboration with Børge Mogensen.

Year built:
1957

Size:
250 sq m

Key materials:
Wood (Oregon-pine, oak, teak and beech)

What makes it unique:
It is the former home of modernist designer Børge Mogensen.

The owners' favourite element:
"Børge's amazing details in Oregon pine that can be found everywhere. And the fireplace. It feels like the entire living room is built around it."

1. The family room and office is the epicentre of the house 2. Art pieces line the windowsill 3. Mobile shades act as wooden peepholes in the front door

1. Bowls, baskets and dinnerware fill the built-in cupboards 2. In the living room, an Eames lounge chair provides a cosy spot to enjoy the fire

1

1

2

3

1. Mogensen's time-tested 2213 sofas with his Spanish chair 2. The house looks out over the countryside 3. The desks are also by Mogensen and the wooden frames by Kaare Klint 4. The winter room, which was added to the house in 1962 by architect Arne Karlsen 5. The open-style kitchen is rumoured to be the first of its kind in Denmark 6. Custom-made grips revamped with new leather handles

5

4

6

Today the architect's no-frills ethos still resonates across the Oregon pine-panelled walls. From tables, cabinets and desks – all solid oak, beech and teak – to drawer handles and window hinges, the elements are made to match.

In the living room, two examples of his most famous design – the 2213 three-seat sofa which was conceived in 1962 and is now a design classic – form the cosiest of corners. The bright winter room, meanwhile, is home to some of the first editions of his J39 chair, or "The People's Chair". Rumour has it the open-style kitchen was the first of its kind in Scandinavia. "I'm not sure if that story is true," admits Ole. "But it's a good one."

Mogensen always considered himself a cabinet-maker, with his mission to produce modest and durable furniture the average working-class Danish family could afford and live with unpretentiously. Here, there are simple, highly functional details everywhere, such as a closable mirror fitted into a wall, movable door blinds and built-in cutting boards in the kitchen.

The Paustians have preserved a piece of architectural history: "The house is a concentrate of what Mogensen typifies in his work. His pieces were not made to be worshipped as a photogenic masterpiece – they were made to be used," says Ole. "Which is also the reason why it would have been dreadful to turn this place into a museum," adds Monika. "It needs to live."

Seeing the potential in an old stable requires creative vision – you would never guess the former purpose of this playful, plaster-covered structure.

15
The sculptural passion project
Maastricht, Netherlands

Valentin Loellmann's home faces the River Meuse on a desirable residential street in Maastricht. A former stable, it had endured a shoddy home conversion before the graduate of the Maastricht Academy of Fine Arts acquired it in 2013. Loellmann, who at the time was establishing a name for himself as a furniture-maker, saw its potential. He was mulling over plans to step into the world of interior design and thought, "What better way is there to show off your skills than the most personal project of building your own home?"

"When I bought the house it was really run down – no electricity, no windows and the roof had fallen down – but it was still a top-tier listed building," he says, noting that securing permission to make major modifications was tough. He decided to take matters into his own hands, working on upgrading the space before permission came through.

Architect:
Originally a horse stable, the structure was transformed into a home by Valentin Loellmann, who added a ground floor and first floor extension.

Year built:
The building was renovated by Loellmann in 2013.

Size:
130 sq m

Key materials:
Mergel stone, Belgian blue stone, oak wood and plaster.

What makes it unique:
Its open layout – there are no doors in the house, apart from on the guest toilet.

The owner's favourite element:
"The reflection of light. The water in the pool bounces light throughout the entire house and off the plaster walls."

2

1. The pool took Valentin Loellmann a week to dig by hand 2. The walls, door frames and ceilings are all coated with white plaster

1. The wooden tables, benches and stools are from Loellmann's atelier; the built-in window seat was also designed by Loellmann

1

1

2

3

1. Calder-inspired mobile made by Loellmann's father in the master bedroom 2. Flooring designed by Loellmann's sister 3. A simple corner in the master bedroom 4. The luminous kitchen features lighting by Serge Mouille 5. The kitchen includes oak work surfaces and brass cabinets

4

5

Thankfully the city of Maastricht was won over by Loellmann's plans, allowing him to go ahead with the renovation.

The overhaul saw the walls, door frames and ceilings coated with white plaster, creating a cave-like effect similar to a Mediterranean stone home. Even on a rainy day the atmosphere remains bright, with light bouncing around the space and onto the timber fixtures – the other key material employed here.

The master bedroom features flooring made from timber slabs (formerly used in the designer's exhibition at Art Basel); long and wide and slightly burnt, they add extra warmth to the property. The wooden tables, benches and stools across the house have come directly from Loellmann's atelier but almost everything else is custom-made: the oak kitchen work surface, brass cabinets and, in the large and open living room, a built-in bench that sits seamlessly in line with the windows above.

The most radical addition to the home, though, is a massive curving window that juts out from an extension on the first floor. "I wanted the shape to reflect the hill so it's just lying on here like a wave," he says. The window enjoys views over the garden, which features a single-lane swimming pool (installed by Loellmann himself) that casts dappled light onto the extended ceiling of the master bedroom. "[The garden] is the most important part of the house – it feels like you are in the middle of nature," he says. "In the morning, light is reflected by the river and in the afternoon, by the pool. Sunlight flows through the house from morning till late evening."

Designed to nurture nature, this concrete structure conceived by Eduard Neuenschwander expertly marries raw materials with the Swiss wilderness.

16
The brutalist bolthole
Gockhausen, Switzerland

Surrounded by emerald-green fields and shaggy pine forests sits the mountainside community of Gockhausen, east of Zürich, created by Swiss modernist architect Eduard Neuenschwander. Designed in the 1960s, the colony of houses and workspaces with their verdant courtyards are testament to the naturalistic approach of the designer, who died in 2013. "He always created the houses and the gardens at the same time," says Matti Neuenschwander of his father. "Most architects just build the houses and the garden is an after-thought but not for him: the plants and the landscaping were just as important."

Today, Gockhausen's two rows of 11 buildings have mostly been converted into private residences. Yet the staggered boxy units with their uniform proportions, glass façades and the intermingling of indoor and out remain a prime expression of the architect's modernist design ideals.

The estate proved to be fertile ground for experimenting with the landscape and it wasn't until 1980 that Eduard built the community's finest residence: the family home in which he lived with his second wife Menchu and their son Christian. Though Menchu says her husband built the house in a hurry (it was autumn and there are traces of fallen leaves in the walls' concrete), it is a spectacular manifestation of the architect's influences – its curved ceiling, exposed concrete walls and sliding glass doors hark back to Le Corbusier – as well as his learnings from the hamlet's other buildings.

Although most surfaces are left exposed, some are rendered smooth with plasterwork; others are puckered and painted white or ochre, the paint always mixed by Eduard himself. "He was concerned with showing the material, the power of concrete," says Matti. "He knew how to use it well." Outside, a curved concrete wall beside the metal front door had been overgrown with ivy, engulfed in nature until Menchu decided she would like to see its form again. "It's a sculpture and it is too beautiful not to show. But that was my husband's speciality: this wilderness."

1

Architect
Eduard
Neuenschwander

Year built
1980

Size
500 sq m

Key materials
Concrete

What makes it unique:
Its amalgamation
of concrete and the
wilderness.

**The owners' favourite
element:** "The heavy
granite round table,
which has a fireplace
in the middle – we
had lots of amazing
dinners around that
fire. We also cherish
the many wooden
pieces made by our
friend Natanel Gluska."

1. Eduard's former architecture studio built in 1964 now functions as a sizeable apartment

1

1. Cosy corner with an unsigned Hans Arp wooden sculpture on the wall 2. Main entrance where autumn leaves can be spotted in the concrete

2

1. A concrete staircase leads down into the open-plan living space in the main residence 2. Vitra's Akari lamp in the living area 3. Living room with Eduard Neuenschwander-designed furniture and lamp 4. Inside the former architecture studio

1

2

3

4

The architect was also a prolific furniture designer and his leather sofas, brass lamps and a wooden table with industrial metal legs sit easily next to a Le Corbusier chaise longue. In the kitchen, a round slab of granite makes a formidable table where friends would often gather during Eduard's lifetime, drawn in by an open fire in its centre. On the walls of the home delicate African textiles – sourced from Menchu's gallery that she ran in the basement of her husband's practice – hang beside Egyptian sculptures, African busts and her husband's botanical sketches. The house is testament to a creative life well lived.

Eduard's work – and this home – was a balancing act: shaping and remoulding to create new habitats that would suit not only people but the flora and fauna around them. "Most modern architects have a narrow outlook," says Matti. "But his was always 360 degrees."

*Set in a cool mountainous village north of Beirut is a traditional
stone house where guests are welcomed as family.*

17
The home from home
Batroun, Lebanon

1

1. Beit Douma is blessed with magnificent views 2. The house is full of inviting seating areas 3. Eclectic decor in the upstairs living space
4. Colourful bed linen and yellow paint brightens up the bedroom

4

2

3

Those who grew up around Batroun, an area an hour or so north of Beirut, know the feel of the old houses here and still carry fond memories of them. Food activist and chef Kamal Mouzawak and fashion designer Rabih Kayrouz are among them – and they're keen to share this feeling with visitors at their guesthouse Beit Douma.

The immaculately rendered 19th-century house is nestled in the breathtaking Batroun Mountains, where there's an agreeable breeze and the average temperature dips to 10C below that endured in Beirut. The traditional Lebanese home impresses with an imposing stone façade and distinctive yellow-and-red shutters. Inside there are lofty wooden ceilings, soaring arched windows and numerous antiques; the effect is of a home from another era. Every inch is carefully conceived and there is a series of connected, airy communal spaces in which to read, rest or eat. The kitchen – a warm and sociable space stocked with fruit grown in the garden – remains the centre of the home where breakfast is enjoyed and neighbours who drop by entertained.

Architect:
Traditional to Lebanon, this style of house is where families from Beirut would spend their summers.

Year built:
Parts date back to the 18th century.

Size:
500 sq m

Key materials:
Stone

What makes it unique:
The traditional property is filled with familiar comforts, with the owners' aims being to remind visitors of their own family homes.

The owner's favourite element:
"It is a very comfortable house with different seating areas that suit different moods and times of the day."

1. Traditional outdoor clay oven 2. Kamal Mouzawak

2

1

1. One of the breezy bedrooms; each of the five is painted in a different pastel shade

1. A Barcelona chair and ottoman by Mies van der Rohe for Knoll and far reaching views of the Batroun Mountains 2. A pendant light illuminates the dining table laden with fresh fruit and other delicacies

1

1. Colourful doorway 2. The downstairs library 3. Vintage furnishings give a homely touch 4. Traditional windows have been painted in a sunny hue
5. Large parties can eat at the shaded table in the garden 6. A modern spiral staircase leads to the top floor

5

6

One reason why the pair's renovation works so well is that while no effort has been spared, much of the expense associated with doing up a house has. The overall ethos is relaxed, comfortable and fuss-free. The property is capacious enough to entertain and – up a modern spiral staircase– it contains five pastel-coloured en-suite bedrooms, each with a view of the surrounding mountains. "The decor in this house is disarmingly simple but refined," says a neighbour. "It's inspired by rustic style and comfort. The most simple objects have a timeless charm: old brass utensils, earthenware, Arabic sofas, flowers, wicker baskets and mismatched tables."

While it may not be any one person's house, this *beit* ("home" in Arabic) really does feel like a home away from home, where Lebanon's legendary hospitality is readily offered and guests are welcomed as family. This is why there are no fancily made beds, logos on towels or a kettle and instant coffee in the rooms. Mouzawak is frank in his disapproval of such things. "Do you have that stuff in your own home?" he asks. "The answer is 'no'. We want Beit Douma to remind you of your grandmother's house."

A Japanese couple managed to elevate the existing character of this once-crumbling building while adding a few elegant touches.

18
The rural homestead
Mashiko, Japan

Architect
Originally built for the Mashiko potter Atsuya Hamada.

Year built
1979

Size
132 sq m

Key materials
Wood, plaster, local Oya stone and *kawara* (clay roof tiles).

What makes it unique:
The home also has a separate studio and kiln.

The owners' favourite element:
"The picture window in the kitchen was a happy accident; Toru got the measurements wrong, ordered a larger piece of glass than needed and decided to knock out some of the wall to accommodate it."

1   2

When Toru and Riho Nihei bought their home in the rural Japanese town of Mashiko, it was in terrible condition. Built in the late 1970s, it hadn't been lived in for a decade and had been damaged by the earthquake that shook the country to its core in 2011. Still, the bones were good and there was plenty of space. "We weren't sure how much work the house needed," says Toru. "But we came here for the location first and foremost."

On closer inspection, it turned out they were able to save the bulk of the wooden-framed house. The roof beams – darkened with a persimmon-fruit stain – have been restored and the partition walls removed to create an open living and dining space.

3

1. Local lava stone provides the backdrop for a modern German woodburner; one of the couple's two rabbits warms itself by the fire 2. A collection of vintage pots and crockery 3. Light streams in through glass doors 4. A woodburner lives outside along with the resident *Ukokkei* (Silkie) chickens

1. The structural wooden frame in the kitchen and dining space was salvaged; the dining table was made from one piece of wood and rests on lava stone

1

1

2

1. The couple prefer a simple interior with a selection of carefully curated pieces 2. A house rabbit makes a dash from the prewar wooden sofa

1. The front doors are from an old *kura* (storage warehouse) 2. Herbs, spices and pickles line the shelves 3. The home is filled with treasured antiques
4. Beams were coloured with a dark persimmon stain 5. *Sumi* (black ink) plaster creates a cocoon-like feel in the hallway 6. Riho is a keen cook

5

6

The interior walls have been covered with *tsuchikabe*, a traditional earth and straw plaster and a dark *sumi* (black ink) plaster.

Mashiko, which sits in Tochigi, a few hours (and a world away) from Tokyo, is one of Japan's most famous pottery towns. Toru comes from the area and runs his antiques business, Pejite, from an old rice warehouse in Mashiko. Although he travels up and down Japan buying furniture for a living, he favours an empty interior. And each piece that does make it into this uncluttered world is carefully considered.

In the living space, a prewar wooden sofa accompanies an Edo-era *tansu* (mobile storage unit) – once used to hold bedding – which now serves as a television stand. Glassware is kept in an old doctor's cabinet and the large dining table is made from a single piece of wood which Toru placed on a base of local lava stone. The same material features as the supporting backdrop for a modern wood-burning stove from Germany. "I love old things but I want to live comfortably too," he says.

The kitchen is a relaxed assemblage of old and new. A professional burner and stainless-steel sink sit alongside vintage crockery, pots and kettles. Riho, a skilled cook, makes her own miso in a wooden barrel that sits outside the back door next to an old-fashioned wood-fuelled *kamado* stove. Here *Ukokkei* (Silkie) chickens roam freely, two tame rabbits sit in front of the stove and a vegetable patch springs to life in warmer weather. "I love to mix traditional and modern living and create something beautiful – that's my thing," says Riho.

The house sits in a picturesque location but Toru and Riho steer clear of rustic whimsy. "People often go for a country look in a setting like this," Toru says. He did, however, remove some jarring features. Unsightly aluminium windows were taken out and he installed a long run of old sliding glass doors along the back of the house, while the entrance doors came from an old *kura* (storage warehouse). The house was previously owned by the late potter Atsuya Hamada, son of the legendary Mashiko ceramicist Shoji Hamada. Atsuya Hamada had built a freestanding studio and kiln on the property where a young potter is now creating pieces for Toru's shop – it's a bucolic scene. Toru and Riho's way of life is as much a work of art as any antique.

In the wilds of Canada this unique property shows that when dealing with tough climatic conditions good design doesn't have to come second.

19
The contemporary cottage
Nova Scotia, Canada

1. The two cedar-shingle structures 2. A wooden doorway 3. A hopefully friendly neighbour

Architect:
MacKay-Lyons
Sweetapple Architects

Year built:
2016

Size:
150 sq m

Key materials:
The spruce wood and
steel structures are
clad in cedar.

What makes it unique:
Its contemporary
take on the area's
vernacular housing.

**The architect's
favourite element:**
The wind trusses.

Canada's dramatic coastlines, deep valleys and wood-lined lakes have long attracted adventurous settlers and, over time, a unique architectural language – one in which resourcefulness, patience and local materiality prevail – has formed. In fact, in a place where howling storms and avalanches are frequent occurrences, practicality is crucial.

This extends to Nova Scotia, whose settler communities didn't care much for flourishes; pragmatism was key for the coast's farmers and fishermen. Their houses were built with "whatever they could get their mitts on," says architect Brian MacKay-Lyons, who has spent decades alongside his firm MacKay-Lyons Sweetapple forging a contemporary style based on such housing stock.

Enter Point House: one of the firm's most spartan expressions of the hardy form, the property was built in 2016. It comprises two structures – a cottage and a boathouse – located down a dirt road on what was traditionally a fishing port. Its rough-sawn spruce wood and structural steel frame is clad in eastern white cedar shingle – with all wood native to the area.

From a distance, it's not immediately obvious what you're looking at. "You really don't know they're not fishing shacks," says MacKay-Lyons. "What makes it look modern is the use of 400-year-old building practices," he says. "What makes it timeless is what makes it contemporary."

1

2   3

1

1. In the living room, a black steel truss is the focal point 2. An Eames lounge chair looks out onto the river 3. Contemporary kitchen 4. A Wishbone chair by Hans J Wegner

This functional minimalism allows for an experience where a traditional wooden stool can sit alongside an Eames lounge chair without seeming out of place, and where coastal wildflowers can grow to the edge of the hemlock terrace. Point House was designed to weather well in place rather than demand perfect grooming.

Sitting in a tidal zone, the house is raised on concrete fins that channel the wind loads and tidal rips beneath it. These use half as much concrete as an ordinary basement. According to MacKay-Lyons, the waves seen through the living room's glass-lined wall are simply the end point of the experience. The real architecture, he says, is in the path between the buildings, up the stairs into a structure defined by an exposed steel truss and a traditional hearth. "The real content is the procession," he says. "You make a banal little house into a big journey."

1

This colourful home was conceived with 'Greekness' at its core and every part of the space was designed to bring the family together.

20
The creative conversion
Athens, Greece

3

Hidden among the narrow streets of Petralona not far from the centre of Athens is a 20th-century home like no other. Petralona House belongs to architect couple Konstantinos Pantasiz and Marianna Rentzou, who set up their practice Point Supreme in 2008 – before which they both worked for Rem Koolhaas's OMA. The pair updated the traditional house from 2013 to 2020 and, when doing so, chose a collision of different colours, materials and forms, blending surrealist ideals with a strong dose of local aesthetics. "Contemporary architecture here tends to be modernist, without much 'Greekness' to it; we wanted to bring back a Greek sensibility," says Pantazis.

1. Konstantinos Pantazis in the back garden 2. Exposed concrete is illuminated by vast windows 3. A seating area and built-in bookcase make use of the split-level space between the stairs

1. Blue swimming pool tiles line the exterior 2. Leafy Brachychiton tree on the ground floor

1

Architect: The early 20th-century property was renovated from 2011 to 2016.

Year built:
1958

Size:
165 sq m

Key materials:
Exposed concrete, ceramic tiles, wood, steel and marble.

What makes it unique:
Thanks to the triangular plot and proximity to neighbouring houses, it has a unusual shape.

The owners' favourite element:
"The house's link with nature – plants and flowers feature throughout and each room has views of the large Brachychiton tree. At night, its leaves produce magical shadows."

1

1. Open-plan kitchen with a view to upper floors

1. Tiles add colour to concrete walls 2. Staircase winds past book-lined walls 3. Bathroom window inspired by designs from Tinos island

In order to achieve this, the couple retained elements including the French shutters, patterned balcony railings (now painted in red, pink and turquoise) and old-fashioned awnings while introducing others; dark-blue pool tiles now cover sections of the exterior and white-and-blue chequered floor tiles, green bathroom walls, mustard window frames, a blood-orange beam and a pink staircase with brass railings decorate the interior. It sounds like a bombardment of the senses but, bathing calmly in the Mediterranean sun, it feels dream-like. "People often ask us, 'Why so many colours?' It's risky but colour is an easy way to add feeling if you manage to find a harmony," says Rentzou.

Inside, the pair have continued with this creative approach: throughout the house, reclaimed furniture resides alongside pieces picked up on their travels. The large dining table in the kitchen was retrieved from outside a museum while multicoloured *listelo* tiles were salvaged from a now-defunct factory. A white-tiled table next to the staircase is a prototype from one of the couple's first projects. "As architects we enjoy using leftover, unused or forgotten pieces. We often find things in factories and shops that have been closed for decades," Pantazis says.

But it is the architects' so-called "public spaces" where the house truly comes into its own. When extending the original ground-storey building to three levels, the couple left a void above the kitchen and living area that looks up to the rest of the home. "It acts as an indoor courtyard where we gather and enjoy simple, everyday moments," says Rentzou. "Greekness is about family life and occasions to celebrate and be together. Our house is designed to encourage this."

Essays
Read all about it

We ask a few of our trusted contacts what truly makes a house a home. Their responses are as varied as their living spaces, but all agree that it is a deeply personal affair.

The concept of home means many things to many people – it is at once universal and incredibly idiosyncratic. So we asked a few top writers, thinkers, designers and architects to reflect on their own living spaces. They talk of the creature comforts they value most – from a good tub to soak in, a *futon* to snooze on and even a furry friend to welcome visitors – and discuss the trials and tribulations involved with turning a blank canvas into a cosy refuge. The voices may hail from Japan and Zimbabwe to Canada and coastal India but these essays share a common theme: your home is what you make of it.

Our relationship with our residences isn't always easy, affable or ideal either (ask our creative director about his battles with the neighbourhood squirrels and he'll confirm that they can drive you nuts). Home-making requires effort but that effort can yield great rewards. So come journey with us and peek through a few windows and behind a few doors to see the diversity of domestic life in all its guises.

The plot thickens

Josh Fehnert

You can't choose your neighbours but there's nothing stopping you from weaving elaborate narratives around them. A new home is a blank canvas – or an empty stage.

I remember sitting daunted and dumbfounded gawping at the sketch of the floorplan for my first house. I wondered: "what can these squiggles reveal about the place I have ploughed my savings into owning?" Later that week, those four walls became my own, but the story of that home – how it leapt off the page and into my life – remained tantalisingly unwritten.

The daubing denoted a modest patch of earth encircling a small terraced house in the middling Midlands town in which I was born. It was rounded by a rickety fence and bearded with an overgrown garden. It was mine in name – then deed – for a few years, anyway. My first house taught me that photos and sketches, illustrative as they can be, confer precious little about how life unfolds in our homes. There's no hint here about the stiff latch, the way the sun hits the windows on a spring morning or the sound the breeze makes in the branches of the silver birch in the front garden.

My theory? That houses are really just ideas, fantasies maybe, until they're inhabited and experienced. They are the staging, the set and the props around which everyday life plays out. Libraries of books offer images and ideas aplenty on how to shape them, refinish, refit and adorn: with furniture, new pictures or a lick of fresh paint. But I'd like to linger on how those walls, streets and city blocks shape us. Houses are plots – literally and figuratively – around which all of our stories are spun.

If like me, and more than half of the world's population, you live in a city or town then you'll recognise that owning a home is also about the streets, blocks and neighbourhoods that surround it. There are the people you live with, those who visit and then the extras. Your fate and mine is inextricably linked to those who fortune deposited next door: the neighbours.

You may share a stud wall with bangers, clatterers, curtain-twitchers or the silent types (seen and seldom heard but *never* noted by the estate agent). I've often

"My partner and I have projected trysts, intrigues and – yes – crimes of every stripe onto our unsuspecting neighbours as they pass unaware"

found it reassuring to know that others are close, even if their lives feel mysteriously far away. Filling in their biographies with far-fetched backstories is a perpetual pleasure: my partner and I have projected trysts, intrigues and – yes – crimes of every stripe onto our unsuspecting neighbours as they pass unaware.

Actually knowing the neighbours can be a pleasure and a comfort but the goodwill can wax and wane. Especially if your neighbours remind you of their presence by waking you up with a shrill giggle or the hum of subwoofer cranking up for a shouty shindig at 3am (shamefully, I've played the role of both noisy neighbour and grumpy grumbler at various times).

In my experience those that you know least well come to take on the roles of pantomime villains, guardian angels or at the very least people who are "up to something". Even the most inscrutable passer-by can be the source of a story and, if there isn't one, we create it, dutifully nestling narratives into the homes and onto the shoulders of those around us. Fearfully enough, you and I are probably also extras in the sullied stage shows of our neighbours' imagining.

Cities promise and deliver a degree of anonymity, excitement and serendipity. But while many leave their villages and quiet suburbs precisely to escape the stony judgement of small-town residents (with long faces and even longer memories), you'll never quite escape human curiosity in a city. It's natural to wonder about the lives lived a wall away, across the street or along the way. We're all intrigued by the human dramas playing out in every house on every street and every city. That intrigue is probably one reason you're reading this, to see what happens behind closed doors.

The adage goes that buying a house is the biggest decision you'll ever make but I'd like to suggest a humble addition to that thought. It's the biggest decision *until* it comes to choosing *how* to live in it. For this, the book you're holding will serve you well with ideas, inspiration and aspiration. After you've moved, decorated or extended you need to decide what's public, private and in what light to show yourself (sometimes literally).

On my desk as I write is a small wodge of printed pages showing a new home, in a pleasant corner of north London, which I'm in the final stages of buying. For now the images are of someone else's home and a small bare garden filled with leafless winter trees. There's a collage of photographs, filled with other people's furniture, fripperies and family pictures. The whole thing is for now an idea – a fantasy. But not for long. Soon it will be filled with stories, noises and gossip about the neighbours. My partner and I will learn to recognise the sound of the wind in the leaves of the plane tree outside and come to know at what time the sun hits the back windows on an autumn evening. We'll hopefully also learn how to jimmy the sticky latch. Once you have a plot of land the story can start a life beyond the printed page – and that's when the plot really thickens.

About the writer
Josh Fehnert is Monocle's deputy editor, oversees the magazine's food and travel coverage and is a regular voice on Monocle 24 radio. He has recently been overheard muttering about the fact that he's *never* moving house again

Carefully does it
Ilse Crawford

The concept of care is central to making our living spaces more, well, liveable. From touch to smell, we need to look beyond the aesthetic and pay attention to all of the senses.

One of the strangest parts of travelling is the new soundtrack to one's life. On a plane there's the clanking drinks trolley with the wobbly wheel, the harsh suction of the toilet, the crackling announcements, the crying babies and the crew gossiping and giggling into the small hours. In hotels you'll hear strangers talking in the corridor, the incessant knocks on the door, the too-loud TV in a neighbouring room, the jovial voices from the bar downstairs late into the night or the muffled sounds of sex through the wall.

Back home the sounds are familiar: you recognise the noise of the coffee grinder in the morning, the heavy-footed cat upstairs, the muffled regularity of the commuter trains whizzing by on their way to London Bridge and the whirring of the electric toothbrush. At night, the sound of a sharp knife on a wooden cutting board, the happy pop of a cork and the comforting click of the light switch bring that warm feeling of everything being right in the world.

But not every sound is welcome of course – there are some noises that are irritating no matter how much they form a part of your everyday reality. The persistent beeps of the washing machine, the dripping tap, the squeal of the hinge next door and the dreaded intercom ("I think it must be for someone else").

So, what makes the difference? It comes down to care. Care is about considering others – about empathy. And it should be a key consideration in the way that the noises in our environments are designed. There needs to be an understanding of where these sounds play out and how they work together. It's not that we want to live in a library-like hush – far from it. But there are some sounds that just put your teeth on edge and it's clear when no thought has been put into the process. It's this that makes the difference. This that we feel instinctively.

The same can be said of touch. It is possible to find things that thrill your fingers, that have integrity and bring comfort to our homes. Fabrics that feel fresh. Materials without chemicals or a coating of plastic. It's a question of priorities and provenance. These days you can find home textiles in organic cotton, linen, nettle and jute – fabrics that are good for both people and planet. Wood floors in stockinged feet are always a joy. It's important to be aware of sourcing – and less obviously coatings. These can also change the feeling of a home. Soap, wax, and oil are so much better than polyurethane lacquers. Sure, they take a little more care, but that's what helps to forge the connection.

Care is central to who we are. To our emotions, to how we feel. To the concept of home. "It is the essence of what it is to be human – to care for the wellbeing of others, to provide care for them and to act with care in regard to them. It embodies everything," says Colin Mayer, Fellow at Hamburg-based research centre The New Institute. Care should underpin all the decisions we make in our homes; indeed it should be the primary concern behind everything we design and make for the places people inhabit in general.

Right now, it isn't. Just think of so-called "care homes". In the formalisation and professionalisation of "care", we've lost sight of the meaning of the word. Generally speaking, these environments – where fluorescent lights, melamine cups and bristly carpets rule – are neither caring nor homely. In the dominant value set today we get lost in the hard and measurable values of rationality, efficiency, functionality, practicality and price. Meanwhile, we denigrate so-called soft values such as care, comfort, beauty and pleasure which are seen as a luxury, not an essential. To create the feeling of home for ourselves and others it is vital that we prioritise care and the unmeasurables – the all-important soft values that make us human.

About the writer
Ilse Crawford is a designer, teacher and creative director. As the founder of Studioilse, she has pioneered humanistic design, always designing for positive mental and environmental impact.

Home is where the bark is
Georgina Godwin

Sometimes our circumstances require us to up sticks and relocate somewhere entirely different. It's the small totems – or furry friends – we take with us that serve as reminders that home is much more than the four walls that enclose it.

The heartbeat is the first sound that any of us ever hear – it is integral to all human life. In Africa, that sound is echoed by the drum, the soul of the community. In my home of Zimbabwe, and all across the continent, drums celebrate many different aspects of life.

The antique version standing outside my front door in Harare was made from the skin of an antelope, dried in the sun and then stretched onto a tall, hollow hardwood frame a hundred years ago. The original vegetable dye patterns have faded over time but the sound still rings out loud and clear. By the time it came into my possession it was no longer used to herald births, deaths or marriages, accompany religious rituals or call up ancestral spirits. It retained only one of its original purposes – to signal the arrival of guests.

My drum was my doorbell, and the rhythmic pounding of my visitors always detonated my faithful dalmatian deep within the house that I'd designed and built – my forever home, I thought. I was confident that my drum doorbell would be the soundtrack to my life and that of my newborn baby, ushering in our friends until we were drummed out, feet first.

When politics and activism forced me to seek sanctuary in London, I found the very British tinny rendition of *London Bridge is Falling Down* at my rental property briefly amusing. I soon grew tired of that, and when I moved to the apartment that would be my home for the next decade I went for the classic *ding-dong*. But there was something missing. With no dogs to welcome visitors, it was clear I needed to relocate to somewhere that could also accommodate a canine companion. Like a tree falling unobserved in a forest, can a visitor arriving without hysterical barking really exist?

And so I moved to a place with room for a bouncy springer spaniel, which clearly needed a suitable doorbell to match. But it was not only me who had moved on – technology too had advanced. My doorbell now has an in-built camera and is linked to an app on my phone. Wherever I am in the world, I can tell the postman to leave the parcel under the bench and, much to her disgust, monitor my teenage daughter's movements. Whether I'm in Australia or Abu Dhabi, it is always reassuring to hear the dog greeting callers in the time honoured way.

I miss my home in Harare every single day. I'd left my book on the bedside table, fully confident I'd return within a few months but instead was declared an "enemy of the State". I haven't been home for many years, and now question if home is indeed a physical place at all. The house and country I yearn for belong to nostalgia, they exist in my memory, while my present is involved with a daily commute through London, the traffic along Baker Street and taking vitamin D for the sunshine I no longer get.

But tucked away under the stairs, safe from the British weather, lives my Zimbabwean drum. And as I walk past, I like to tap out a rhythm that reminds me of my former life. Though I may be in a thriving metropolis where technology monitors my every movement, there is something deeply ancient and spiritual about this simple act that speaks to my emotions – and excites the dog.

About the writer
Georgina Godwin is Monocle 24's literary editor. She was banned from Zimbabwe and declared an "enemy of the state", after setting up the nation's first independent radio station. Her springer spaniel is called Bella.

Concrete plans

Richard Spencer Powell

We know that gardens are good for us, but we often forget they can be hard work. Occasionally it pays to take the less is more approach.

The common trajectory of home ownership in London starts with a studio flat and, if you're fortunate, culminates in an old brick terrace house with a tiny garden. Outdoor space at last, a haven for a rare sunny day in an inclement climate. But gardens are challenging and require some mystical skills – what even are green fingers? They don't teach horticulture in school, it's not a life skill you pick up like cooking or one that's as easy to assimilate. In short, growing a courgette is a lot harder than cooking one.

When I moved into my house in 2010, I was enthused by the prospect of planting, growing, mowing and pruning. Garden tools from Germany were assembled, hose systems researched, planters neatly placed – even fashionable gardening gloves were considered. The first task was to tackle the lawn: a perennial quagmire or tundra depending on the season. So I toiled in the soil, sowed, watered and waited. Several weeks later a green haze began to materialise through the topsoil; a month later, a full lawn. My first success but sadly not my only lawn. I have had four lawns now – replanted once every two years or so. I have tried two types of grass seed, including one meant for shady areas, and laid turf twice. On each occasion, over time, the lawn turns to a mossy, scruffy, weed-ridden patch of misery. It's a war of attrition with the combined forces of shade, clay, tree roots, leaf mould and squirrels winning every conflict.

Which is why, in the end, I concreted over my garden and watched as the bemused squirrels searched for their buried nuts. To be clear, I didn't convert it into a carpark; the concrete is more akin to stone decking, with beds cut into it. It is laid out on several levels and will eventually have moss and ground-covering plants in between its cracks and crevices. Some of the old flora has been retained and replanted and it is happily verdant. Evergreens, acers, ferns and sumacs fill the borders with grasses, reeds and bamboo plugging the gaps. There's even a potted silver birch tree to sit under.

It was a brave decision to forgo the grass – one I'm not sure John at number four appreciates yet – but concrete is a warm material, hard under foot yet soft on the eye. And the beautiful palette fondly reminds me of trips to Tokyo, of the grey city surrounded by green farms and fields. My garden is modern, it is designed and it is functional. Pots can be moved as the temperature and seasons change, the ground can be swept and even vacuumed. There is hardly any need for tools or maintenance and it looks as good in winter as it does in summer. I don't have green fingers but I do have a green and grey garden.

About the writer
Richard Spencer Powell is Monocle's creative director. To those who know him, it will come as no surprise that he took the neat approach to gardening – he is famous throughout the office for his fastidiously organised bookshelves.

It's only natural
Zoe Chan Eayrs

We once constructed our homes exclusively from the raw materials found in the surrounding area – we could learn a lot from returning to a more organic approach to nesting.

Growing up, I relentlessly re-arranged my bedroom in a quest to find the perfect composition. I'm often reminded of this when I see our dog nestling into his blanket, kicking the folds until everything is just right for him to settle down and finally take a nap.

Surely we all have this nesting instinct? It might be buried deeper in some than in others, but ultimately we once would have made our home in huts or caves, as a bird instinctively makes their nest. We would have found the perfect spot – safe, sheltered and close to the things we needed for survival. We would have foraged for the right materials from the local environment and created something that would suit the climate we lived in. Our homes would have been of the ground – made of the same natural materials that constituted the surrounding landscape.

We seem to have forgotten this. Today, we construct our homes with foams and fillers, chemicals, varnishes, adhesives and toxic paints, membranes, mastics and plastics. These chemicals leach into our internal environments and we add to them with our cleaning products, cosmetic sprays,

and cooking fumes. Noxious gasses and volatile organic compounds float through our air and into our bodies. How did this happen and why do we not question the fabric of our most sacred space?

The basic function of a home is to provide us with safety from the elements and our surrounding environment – so what can we do about it? Make your home natural, make it breathable, make it organic, make it with local materials, make it to suit the climate – ideally make it yourself. And don't forget to open the windows.

Choose locally sourced timber, wood fibre board and cork; opt for clay plaster and clay paint as well as lime plaster, limecrete and lime mortars; select natural oils and recycled glass aggregate, cob, earth, and stone; and use straw and carbon-negative hemplime. Reject chemicals and plastics. Choose to be curious.

About the writer
Zoe Chan Eayrs is one half of home-makers Chan + Eayrs. They champion a slow and natural approach and source, design and make everything from scratch – from finding the right site to choosing the perfect teacup.

The high life
Nolan Giles

There are few greater pleasures in life than a sun-drenched coffee break on your own balcony – something the smart residents of Zürich cottoned on to a long time ago.

The balcony is the sunny outdoor room synonymous with Swiss summertime. From ornate neoclassical homes to smooth concrete-walled modernist flats, the architectural fabric of Zürich is one that is marked magnificently with myriad balconies. For residents of the city – like myself – they provide the perfect spot to take in the gentle Föhn breeze, which rolls down from the alps, across our shimmering lake and into this prosperous city whenever the mercury soars.

Cool and practical (a bit like the Swiss) these beautiful balconies cling to buildings across the city and tend to be finely shaded and furnished with an individuality that reflects their owner's taste. Capped off with a tasteful awning, a perfectly presented patch of white and red geraniums, or just an allowance for a neighbour's unkempt vine to swing lazily over it, these objects of architecture take on their own soul in harmony with the laidback quality of life citizens enjoy.

In the summer, visitors watch with envy as locals swing open wooden louvers or wind up their rolling shutter to let the daylight pour into their handsome homes. Stepping onto a spacious balcony, freshly brewed coffee in hand and surveying the scene below, it's clear to see why those above are catching the admiring glances of their poor pavement-stranded onlookers.

It's a fine life to be blessed with a generous balcony that stimulates all the senses. Enveloped in the aroma of your sky-high herb garden, enjoying views of the city and the fresh lake air on your skin, it's simply the only place to spend a summer's morning. It's no surprise then, that Zürich's builders enjoy a roaring trade in constructing "bolt-on balconies". This local innovation sees the retrofitting of new balconies onto older blocks in just a matter of days.

As an observer of good architecture it's safe to say (with maybe a hint of bias) that Zürich's balconies put their poorly planned cousins in larger cities to shame. While others waste their balconies as disposable spaces for extra storage, here in Zürich the balcony is the most celebrated room in the house. And when they look this good why shouldn't they be? We at MONOCLE are firmly in praise of a zesty Zürich balcony.

About the writer
As a senior editor at Monocle, Nolan Giles commissions, writes and edits articles with a special focus on design, architecture and fashion. He is also the presenter of *Monocle on Design*, a weekly podcast about the creative industries.

Mix and match

Byron and Dexter Peart

Our homes should be a reflection of our personal taste, tell our stories through their design and we should celebrate their differences.

As the winter snow melts, the sun sets later and the birds make their migration back north, there is something incredibly heartwarming and optimistic about springtime in Montréal. From the windows of our homes at Habitat 67 – Moshe Safdie's brutalist modular masterpiece, comprised of 354 stacked concrete boxes – we observe the glittering lights of the city and monitor the changing of the seasons.

We find ourselves adjusting our homes to reflect the natural shifts taking place beyond our windows. Today more than ever, our interior spaces have become the setting for introspection, rejuvenation and replenishment – and we have become acutely aware of how our homes continue to function as living organisms; ones that allow us to cultivate a better sense of joy, peace, comfort and security.

As inseparable twins, we have always lived extremely close to one another, so perhaps it's no surprise that for more than a decade we have chosen to live in the same housing development. While many of our past life experiences have been shared, our homes distinctly reflect the independent

evolutions of our personal style, taste and the separate life narratives we have constructed with our families.

Dexter's home is very much a high-spirited family home, reflective of his and his wife Maria's fast-paced professional and parental lives coupled with the often animated lifestyle of their pre-teen daughters. The stacked bookcases and well-adorned walls tell the stories of their far-flung travels. In contrast, Byron and his husband Stefan's interior aesthetic marries the couples' appreciation for the functionality and timelessness of Bauhaus design, with their eccentric collection of art pieces and trinkets – all rooted in tradition, colour, and style.

For us, home has always been a plural experience – informed by the places we previously lived in and the locations we travelled to, the food we ate and the moments we shared. As Jamaican-Canadian twins growing up in the suburbs of Ottawa, we absorbed diverse cultural perspectives and stitched together a unique sense of belonging that felt both beautiful and natural to us. In our childhood home, the scent of the carved-wood furniture reminded us of our parents' homeland. The food our mother prepared appealed to our roots, creating a welcome link to our ancestors. Meanwhile, our father would gather us around the dining room table for lively debate about the latest ideas or cultural trends. We cherished this suburban upbringing.

Over the years, as we've created our own homes in Montréal, we've been mindful of designing spaces that help foster meaningful connections with the people (and places) that are nearest and dearest to us. We believe that decorating your home should be a natural process – a well-considered home that's comfortable and reflective of personal tastes, comprising the travel finds and family heirlooms of all of the inhabitants. Recognising that, even if our homes feel different, smell different, or look different in some ways, when designed with intent they all have the power to open up room for healthy human experiences and the increased wellbeing of our families, communities and neighbours.

About the writers
Twin brothers Byron and Dexter Peart are the co-founders of Goodee, a homeware brand that works exclusively with products that make a strong social or environmental impact. They aspire to bring together good design and good purpose.

Beauty sleep
Fiona Wilson

Unlike its 1980s namesake, the Japanese futon is surprisingly comfortable and the ultimate space-saving solution.

Long before Marie Kondo and her declutterering acolytes appeared on the scene, traditional Japanese homes had already solved the issue of how to deal with unwanted stuff by having almost no furniture and few posessions. Aside from the odd *tansu* (wooden chest), low table and a legless *zaisu* chair or two, houses were no more than a series of empty spaces partitioned by sliding doors. Rather than being a lifestyle choice, minimalism was built into the architecture itself.

Instead of hulking Western-style beds – which are a disaster for soft tatami flooring anyway – the Japanese slept on *futon*: layered cotton mattresses that could be folded away during the day and hidden from view. And many still do. While beds are far more common in Japanese homes than they used to be, the *futon* is still popular, sold everywhere from Muji to Takaokaya – a Kyoto company that has been hand-making *futon* since 1919.

To Western ears, the word "futon" likely evokes a rudimentary sofa bed with a wooden-slatted base. Although the Japanese *futon* was the inspiration for this 1980s invention, the two bear only a passing resemblance. The Japanese version is strictly speaking a full set-up with mattress (*shikibuton*) and a quilt (*kakebuton*) on top. It is pulled out at night, laid out directly on the floor – sometimes with an extra layer underneath – and folded away in the morning.

This foldable mattress makes perfect sense for compact homes where space is in short supply (apartments were always built with cupboards large enough to store bedding). Once it has been stowed away, the room is freed up for other purposes during the day. Several *futon* can be laid out in even a small space and parents often sleep in one room with their young children. There's no chance of toddlers falling out of bed and they happily sprawl next to their parents.

The whole thing does require some maintenance. To keep them clean and free of mould – a big consideration in Japan's humid summers – sleeping mats are hung out to get rid of mites and moisture. On sunny days, it's a common sight to see them suspended from balconies, held firm with an oversized peg designed especially for the purpose. A *futon tataki* (beater) is a key piece of kit and there are driers designed specifically for them.

> "The Japanese have been sleeping on some version of the *futon* for centuries. Easily rolled up and carried, the sleeping mat offered easy mobility in more peripatetic days"

About the writer
Fiona Wilson is Monocle's senior Asia editor. She has lived in Tokyo for many years and travelled the length and breadth of Japan. She resides in a Western-style apartment but dreams of tatami mats and a solid eight-hour sleep on a proper *futon*.

It's also an eco-friendly product – and not only because it's made of natural materials: once it's worn out, a good maker will turn an old *futon* into *zabuton* floor cushions.

The Japanese have been sleeping on some version of the *futon* for centuries. Easily rolled up and carried, the sleeping mat offered easy mobility in more peripatetic days. Today, many are made by machine though a handmade *futon* is a pleasure, particularly one made by a master craftsman. Hisayoshi Nohara, one of the best in the business, has been making the mattresses since the 1970s and sells them from his bedding shop in Kanagawa. He skillfully layers the cotton before encasing it in a cover and securing it at strategic points with a final few stitches. Nohara is a passionate believer in the virtues of the *futon* and its ability to ensure a good sleep and a healthy back.

Any visitor to Japan who is hankering to try one only has to spend a night at a traditional *ryokan* inn. Some newcomers are stubbornly (and mistakenly) resistant to the idea, thinking it equates to camping out on a hard floor. On the contrary, a well-made *futon* and a pillow stuffed with buckwheat chaff are usually a guarantee of a good night's sleep.

Take a seat

Rolf Hay

The best furniture designs combine functionality, sustainability and comfort without compromising on beauty – they may just take a little while for the general public to warm to them.

If we begin by looking at some of the best chairs designed over the course of the last century, it's interesting to note that the majority of them were not immediately accepted by the populace. Quite the contrary: these now iconic pieces were often failures of their own time, and all because they offered something different to what was already in existence. Considering this, you might be inclined to conclude that when striving to create a classic, all you need to do is to buck the trend.

This is not the case, of course, as the original nature of these chairs is ultimately only one aspect of what makes them extraordinary. Personally,

I don't believe there is any great quality in making something different simply for the sake of it. But I do believe it can be a good starting point for crafting something innovative, something that improves upon what's already out there.

"Better" can mean many things. It can mean more environment friendly, comfortable or beautiful – it can also mean less expensive. There is no doubt that many classics came from a desire to give people greater access to high-quality design. The key to this was making new use of existing technologies and methods, re-imagining tools and materials in ways that were compatible with industrial production.

Take the Thonet No 14 Chair, a revolution that used steam-bent beech to create a valuable seat in a less expensive way. The same goes for pioneers Ray and Charles Eames, who insisted on innovating with new materials like moulded plywood and fibreglass, producing beautiful items for a mass market. And the Danish design heroes Hans J Wegner and Børge Mogensen? Both were driven by the desire to create well-conceived products for normal families, school children – for everyone.

These values, and a commitment to clean and affordable production, are certainly at the heart of Hay. It goes without saying that we, as furniture manufacturers today, carry an extended responsibility for the future of our children to create products that achieve a much higher standard of sustainability than those of the past, that utilise responsible materials and production methods. But I also believe that there is much more to ensuring the longevity of a product.

Beyond their innovation, originality and resourcefulness, the classics of design history were distinguished by their comfort, elegance and beauty. And the core values for creating a good chair remain completely unchanged. A good chair must touch us and make us want to touch it. Qualities of form, line, texture and shape are harder to quantify than sustainable achievements – but they are equally essential components when building something that inspires us to care for it. It is about creating something that will, come what may, stand the test of time.

About the writer
Rolf Hay co-founded Danish design brand Hay with his wife Mette in 2002. As the mischievous creative director of Hay Furniture and Hay Lighting, he continues to keep things interesting, working tirelessly against the staid and sometimes static nature of the design industry.

Living on the edge
Tishani Doshi

Building your home next to the ocean can bring its own challenges but once you learn how to adapt to the rhythms of the landscape and accept that you will have to get up close and personal with the local wildlife, it can be a truly enchanting experience.

I was certain I did not want air-conditioning. I did not want a wi-fi router. No television, no doorbell, no post. Thanks but I'd rather not be reached. I had a vision of lying on an antique chaise lounge, three dogs on the floor, two wooden fans spinning from the ceiling, the air filled with their soft click-clack soundtrack. I'd nurture a vegetable garden, transform into an unfussy but brilliant cook, learn the names and subspecies of birds and plants. All from my house by the sea.

The sea holds the deep future and the past, makes and remakes the world with its rhythmic breathing. When you put a conch up to your ear, you can hear the whole living world. It reminds you of the breath inside you. Imagine living inside the conch, the sea at your front gate, the comfort of its ever-present charge and retreat, charge and retreat. This is what I expected coastal living would be – a kind of womb-like existence.

I was fed up with the world. With its noise and speed. I was committed to the idea of poetry and I wanted to live it, not just on the page, but in every room of my life.

Where we live, on a rural spit of beach in South India, on the east coast between Chennai and Pondicherry, my husband and I are adrift. The problem with having no TV, post or doorbell is that the news cycle reaches you anyway but no one comes to collect the rubbish. The fishing hamlets with their jumbles of colourful boats and nets are besieged with empty bottles and discarded crisp packets. The nearest rubbish bin is an hour's drive away.

Some mornings I wake with the sound of Tamil film songs throbbing across the air. The neighbourhood temples prefer pop to devotional, and because there are no buildings to absorb the noise, sound travels freely through fringes of coconut

"We measure seasons by the insects and critters that share our home. February brings tree frogs. July, the first wave of migrating butterflies. November is all mayflies, midges and mosquitoes"

and palmyra. Not to be outdone, the neighbourhood church has installed a computerized clock that chimes loudly at four minutes to the hour, as if to prove they're ahead of the times. The loudspeaker is the small town's rejoinder to the world for being small.

Living here is magic. As soon as you turn off the highway, you are among egrets and kingfishers, electric green bee-eaters and hoopoes. The land claims you. Soft undulating dunes, a glimmering strip of backwater that opens onto the sea. Stubby neem and cashew razoring horizontally across the sand because the salt air won't allow them to grow upwards. After the monsoons, it is all a kingdom of unimaginable lushness. Time alters. Expands and nets its arms around your entire life. Gathers you into a centre.

When I was nine, I nearly drowned in the Bay of Bengal. Perhaps it's why I've always wanted to live close to it. To remind myself of the dangers. I remember feeling the water at my feet grow suddenly cold, pulling me away from the shore and my family. It was a small riptide that eventually spat me out, but for years after I dreamt of a giant wave taking us all away, twirling us upwards into the sky like a reverse tornado.

After the Indian Ocean tsunami in 2004, I drove down the coast to see the wreckage. We had just bought the land, but our dreams of building the house were now on hold. There were too many what-ifs? Cyclones, rising sea levels, a central government coal plant threatening to spring in a bloom of ugliness.

To live by the sea is to accept fragility. We measure seasons by the insects and critters that share our home. February brings tree frogs. July, the first wave of migrating butterflies. November is all mayflies, midges and mosquitoes. Different armies of ants patrol throughout the year, along with geckos and baby bats who love nesting behind the mirrors. This January, after the jungle around the house had been pruned, bronze-back tree snakes made homes in our bathrooms, looking more terrified than we were to encounter one another. "Treat them as honoured guests," my wildlife conservationist friend said. We are all guests by the sea.

When we first moved in, another friend had suggested air-conditioning the whole house to improve the acoustics. "But what about the poetry?" we asked. I cannot remember when we succumbed. But one day we bought a wi-fi dongle because standing on the bathroom ledge to catch phone signal became too much. We installed an air-conditioner in the studio for summer when everything becomes strangulated.

We created our first boundary and then we kept making them. Closed all the windows and doors before dusk to keep the bugs out. Oiled the door hinges regularly instead of waiting for them to fall off. Every night, we retire to the studio. The noises are kept at bay – the howling dogs, the rival temple and church, all the majesty and tenderness of the sea. It has made life easier. There is still poetry – but now we sleep.

About the writer
After a failed career as a scuba diver, Tishani Doshi turned to poetry and dance. Her most recent book is a novel, *Small Days and Nights*, shortlisted for the RSL Ondaatje Prize. She lives on a beach in Tamil Nadu in southern India with her husband and dogs.

Soak it up
Lou Stoppard

There to share our most personal and private moments, our bathrooms are the unsung heroes of our homes. Lock the door and breathe out.

The bathroom is the best room in the house. I say this partly for aesthetic reasons, drawn to the graphic lines of tiles, the reassuring sense of containment and order in rows of sweet-smelling bottles. But also because of the bathroom's versatility, its remarkable potential for a broad spread of tasks; showering, soul searching, flossing, philosophising. It serves a plurality of purposes that range from the mundane, the base (the disgusting, even) to the profound, the transformative, the spiritual. Depending on why one heads there, and how one makes use of the time, one can exit a bathroom merely relieved. Or one can leave realigned, therapised by time spent alone – truly alone – and bared, for the household bathroom offers little opportunity for pretence.

One of my favourite artworks is Wayne Thiebaud's 1965 painting "Woman in Tub". In some ways, it's more about the tub than the woman: the bulk of the canvas is given over to the straight sides of the bath. The woman's body is invisible. We only see her neck and head, which lolls back against the top of the tub. Her eyes look forward but are tilted up and seem unfocused (or maybe I imagine them to be based on my own bath-time meditations, hours spent looking at, but not really taking in, the ceiling). Bathing women litter art history but Thiebaud's painting, to me, is the greatest example of the sensation of bathing – of sinking, of reappearing, of the many things one does. It's the genius of the woman's expression, which falls somewhere between peaceful and stoic, hopeful and resigned. I see in her face an acknowledgment of the enormity of living; the potentials, the risks, the overwhelming impossibility of knowing whether you're getting it right. It is an incredibly profound painting, if you care to see it, just as any bathroom can offer an incredibly profound experience if you allow it.

I am a dedicated swimmer, so bathrooms have also meant communal changing, a sea of curves and patches of hair, angled away. They have meant hot feet against cool tiles in the summer, on holiday, sand from someone else's costume already lining the tub, a glass of wine by the sink. They have been

spaces to comfort friends, to regroup and to call someone to tell them that you miss them.

One becomes oneself in part through the myriad places one dwells, and the moods and norms there. I think if I looked back and tried to match profound realisation to geographic position, I would land often at bathrooms; those breaks, the heart-to-hearts, the times when I have, for just a minute, slipped away. Indeed, the bathroom is where one goes to briefly release oneself from the smother of humanity, the pressure of being a responsive person; the place to recoup before returning to the parade.

It's put beautifully in Miranda July's short story *Something That Needs Nothing* in which she writes: "I politely excused myself. In the powdery warmth of the bathroom I felt euphoric. Being alone suddenly felt wild. I locked the door and made a series of involuntary, baroque gestures in the mirror. I waved manically at myself and contorted my face into hideous unlovable expressions [...] I was experiencing a paroxysm of selfhood."

The very purpose of a bathroom is transformation – dirty to clean, bursting to empty, dressed to naked to dressed again. One thing to another. Happiness can be a side product, but the real gift is the chance to reckon with oneself during the pursuit of revival. The solutions, the insights, can creep slowly, enveloping you like warm water. Or they come fast, a flash when you see yourself in the mirror; the paroxysm of selfhood July describes.

Sometimes I enter my own bathroom in the morning, face pillow-marked, eyes still full of sleep, and emerge made-up, presentable, ready to go somewhere. I am altered. Other times nobody but me notices the shift. I go in searching and leave something else entirely. Toes and fingers sometimes wrinkled. Skin still slightly wet.

About the writer
Lou Stoppard is a British writer and curator based in London. Her latest book, *Pools: Lounging, Diving, Floating, Dreaming: Picturing Life at the Swimming Pool*, is out now and published by Rizzoli.

Display of affection
Gianfranco Chicco

Objects needn't be rare, expensive or have artistic merit for them to be valuable – putting our favourite items on display can spark joy every time they catch our eye.

The nature of my work requires intense periods on the road followed by stints working from home – I've barely spent any time in an office over the last decade. It always feels great to come back to my London flat but if I spend extended periods of time there even the smallest thing can rub me up the wrong way. The latest culprit was the rubbish bin: inherited from the previous tenant, it spent seven years opposite the table where I work, a constant presence in my field of vision.

That is, until one day a glimpse of it made me realise that I had been tolerating it for too long. It was large, faulty and ungracious. After a deep dive into the world of domestic waste containers, I now have one that's half the size, features a silent mechanism and is the result of thoughtful design. Out of all the things that needed addressing, was this an absolute priority you might ask? Yes. The bin is always visible and serves an important function multiple times a day. Even after a few months, the new model makes me smile every time I notice it.

Inspired by this simple fix I made some other changes around the house. I made my favourite tea bowls available to be handled on a daily basis. The copper tea caddies I had in a cupboard are now on view next to the sofa. My old Hasselblad sits on a shelf where I can admire its pragmatic build, or grab it for an impromptu photoshoot in the park across the street.

However, one has to be careful not to overdo it. I tend to follow the tradition observed in old Japanese houses, where it's considered in bad taste to show off all your precious possessions at once, favouring instead the rotation of a few things in harmony with the seasons or matching a particular occasion. I have yet to master the fine balance between stimulation and saturation, but at least that hideous bin is out of my life forever.

About the writer
Gianfranco Chicco is an experience designer, writer, and Japanophile. He once had breakfast in Tokyo, lunch in London, and dinner in Milan in the same day – which resulted in severe jet-lag and a cancelled credit card.

Community
Come together

No man is an island, and very few of us live in complete isolation. We consider how architecture and urban planning can help foster healthier and happier interactions with those who build their homes alongside our own.

More than half the world's population now lives in cities and this means the way we build homes, interact with our neighbours and even cater for different generations is more important than ever. Whether you settle in a towering apartment block or a bushy suburban cul-de-sac, your life will be coloured by your connections with others – and life can be better when you get to know the people next door.

We begin with some concrete (and brick) examples and an exploration into communal living. We hop from the social housing blocks of Singapore to a retirement complex in the south of France to learn the value of smart shared-use developments across the world. What all these projects have in common is an awareness that architecture can enhance our quality of life. They also show how the developments that find the right balance between personal privacy and public spaces in which to mix can bring out the best in all those who call them home.

We also profile six of our favourite 'hoods – each one a benchmark for building better communities. Good design plays a pivotal role in providing housing that the occupants are proud to look after but another ingredient is the human history and local culture, which tempt new arrivals and keep these city corners fresh. Some of these neighbourhoods were built with communities in mind, others have happened to hit on the formula organically – all of them are well worth a wander.

Notes on community
In good company

As our cities reach peak population, the need for clever housing solutions is becoming ever pressing. While some may suggest that vast apartment blocks can lead to a lack of community, we believe the opposite: good design can, and does, facilitate togetherness. Here we profile eight housing developments where the structures themselves promote neighbourly love.

1. An open staircase at the back of a Bremen Cube 2. Residents Günter and Vera Runken on their sun-drenched terrace 3. Annemarie Hacker has lived on the Gewoba development since 1957 4. The Bremen Cube's exterior 5. Renate Andreas and dog Aska are fans of their modular, cube-shaped apartment

① Bremen Cube
Bremen
Creating extra space for residents within a confined footprint doesn't have to involve erecting lofty apartment blocks. The Bremen Cube demonstrates how multiple low-rise buildings can be integrated to increase density without detracting from an area's character. These cubes don't compromise on the quality of life for tenants either – the homes within boast generous ceiling heights and spacious balconies for all to enjoy.

4

5

Home might be where the heart is but ultimately it is our wider community that fosters our most rewarding domestic experiences. Whether you live in a tiny rural village or a colossal apartment block, few of us are truly at home in isolation. And it's city living where design for community has advanced most in recent years – with good architects and urban planners doing their best to forge successful developments that emphasise a kinship between those that inhabit them.

Innovation has come from necessity and might be best represented in the Southeast Asian city-state of Singapore where land space is scarce (and expensive) and a population of diverse ethnicities all live together. To deal with this, the government's **Housing & Development Board (HBD) (6)** took serious strides in the 1960s to deliver community homes en-masse. They looked skyward and formed what might best be described as villages in the sky – vertical satellite towns that offered shared spaces (on rooftops as well as at street level), outdoor food courts and bustling markets. Strategically positioned on public transport networks that linked these communities to the Central Business District, they defined urban living in Singapore.

Walking around an HBD apartment building today (where 80 per cent of the city's population now resides), you'll see how those 1960s roots of experimental social living have grown into thriving developments with community at their core. Families convene at their block's play parks while green-thumbed residents tend to shared vegetable gardens. At night "uncles" and "aunties" (the names Singaporeans affectionately call their elders) gather in semi-outdoor food halls, cooling off with a Tiger beer while playing cards together. Residing in a small apartment in land-scarce Singapore is an accepted way of life – but only because these sites offer such a rich, social lifestyle.

A lack of land in cities is an issue the world over and, as people moved to urban areas after the Second World War, architects pioneered with new materials such as concrete to deliver projects that changed the way we thought about living. Famously, the **Barbican Estate (7)** –built in a bombed-out patch of central London between 1965 and 1976 – showed that aspirational city living no longer had to be about owning a private townhouse with a garden. Here the luxuries were convenience to the city's amenities and being around like-minded neighbours. For Barbican residents (back then and now) socialising plays out across handsome shared gardens and courtyards.

Another lesser-known example of this changing ideal of community living can be found in Vienna: **Wohnpark Alt-Erlaa (8)** (which roughly translates as "Park Residences Alt-Erlaa") was designed by architect Harry Glück in the late 1960s. His "residential park" concept was built around a closeness to nature and the possibilities for forging communities. One essential factor in its enduring success is aesthetics: the design is remarkably intriguing. Apartments – which feature generous balconies with ample space for lush planting – terrace skywards on towers that resemble pyramids, allowing sunlight to stream into each of the homes. The upper-storey flats have smaller balconies but the stunning views across Vienna and the nearby woodlands make up for it.

The most important architectural factor, however, is that it encourages a communal life for all. The floor plans of the Alt-Erlaa towers are purposely wide and deep so that the interior spaces beyond the apartments can be used for social clubs, leisure centres or whatever the residents wish for. On top of each building is a swimming pool and sauna while tennis courts and mini-golf courses are found on the ground floors. Using the space for free, the residents have formed more than 30 clubs – from photography to ballroom dancing. Tenants of the 3,000 plus homes also enjoy access to two kindergartens, a children's day care centre, a church, three schools, two medical centres, restaurants and a shopping centre. It's for this reason that new residents can wait for years for a home to become available.

Well-designed apartment buildings tend to attract demand but their architecture can also instil a sense of pride in those lucky enough to dwell in them. This has certainly been the case at the **Lausanne apartment building (2)** in São Paulo – a 1958 mid-century gem designed by German-Brazilian architect Adolf Franz Heep. In the late 2010s and early 2020s, residents took it upon themselves to restore the decaying building to its original glory. The work included fixing magnificent mosaics, replanting multiple flowerbeds and the careful repainting of a mural by Brazilian artist Clóviz Graciano that adorns the building's curved entrance walls – all co-funded by residents.

"Without the community support none of this work would be possible," says Regina Ponte, who led the project and to this day collects monthly maintenance payments from those who live here. Ponte saw beauty in the faded hues of Lausanne's colourful system of window shutters that gracefully covers its façade (today resplendent in fresh pastel reds, greens and creams). She made it her mission to convince tenants that it was their time to restore this modernist marvel and raised the funds and goodwill to do so. Clearly the effort is one that captured the imagination of the community and it is a story mirrored in many other modernist apartment buildings, which today attract a discerning, design-loving crowd.

While we've harked on about handsome high-rises up until this point, winning community developments don't have to be skyscrapers. Sometimes the addition of a big brutish block can destroy a vibe in a leafy low-set neighbourhood. Yet as cities expand in size, it's important to maximise the land within its suburbs to prevent the inevitable issues arising from urban sprawl. The German city of Bremen combated this problem with a daring prototype for a low-rise apartment building, which has proved that densification in the suburbs need not detract from the quality of life or character of a neighbourhood. Here, the **Bremen Cube (1)**, developed by housing provider Gewoba and architecture firm Lin in 2017, has added homes to the urban fabric with a minimal footprint. The design itself is a clever one: consisting of modular units that can be built off-site and formed quickly in a neighbourhood (avoiding noisy construction disturbances), it has been dubbed as "fast, smart and small," by the developers. In the years since construction, the four-storey structures already feel at home here – as do the tenants.

While large property companies tend to be responsible for building most modern apartment blocks, sometimes the most innovative ideas that foster better communities come from those more personally involved. Completed in 2018, **La Borda (3)** is one of Barcelona's first co-housing projects. It was designed by and for its inhabitants with the help of Lacol, a co-operative of 14 architects, five of whom are also residents. While occupants had to sacrifice a little private space, the development offers well-designed communal components including a utility room and a play area for children, as well as a kitchen and dining space for multi-tenant meals. "The idea is that your home is the whole building," says Pol Massoni from Lacol architects. The development

also offers ideas for other cities and countries to draw on when housing an ageing population, a particular problem in Spain. "For us it was important to be mixed with people of different ages," says Rosa Mestres, a retired nursery teacher who lives in La Borda with her husband. "Life in the common areas is fantastic; all the children know us," she says.

As this story illustrates, the best community buildings are those that bring together a diverse set. It's something that families, who in years' past may have opted for a detached suburban dwelling, are increasingly coveting. **79&Park (5)** designed by starchitect Bjarke Ingels' firm Big, is home to many families (and singles and elderly), who've shirked suburban seclusion in favour of being close to others.

The Stockholm-based structure appears as a wooden hillside that blurs borders between living spaces and the greenery that surrounds them. Ingels says that the development aims to find the "humane edge between nature and building", promoting a warm, community-driven model for urban living. Flexible property sizes attract a diverse social and generational mix, while the smart shape of the wooden structure provides space for amenities such as a deli, a hairdresser and a nursery. Neighbours are closer here than they would be in suburbia but this doesn't feel like a typical apartment block. There's a leafy, relaxed atmosphere at 79&Park and one that has made it Stockholm's most lusted-after addresses.

Finding a spot to settle into as we approach our silver years is a matter designers and architects are paying great attention to these days. The global proportion of people passing 60-plus years in age is rising dramatically and future retirees are going to live longer. What's important for them is continuing to enjoy vibrancy in these years. Aged care homes and retirement villages are not alluring places for seniors and better designed solutions, enhanced by ideas about community building, are springing up across the globe. In Copenhagen a development called Future Sølund by CF Møller Architects is proposing a new type of living for the ageing. Yes, the sprawling development will have nursing-home units to care for the infirm but also hundreds of houses for families as well as student's quarters, a nursery, a barber's shop, squares and

Lausanne building
São Paulo
Successful housing developments tend to attract like-minded tenants. This is most certainly the case at the Lausanne building in São Paulo, where a creative cast of residents have made the most of the cleverly enclosed balconies and double-height ceilings. Their talents have also been applied to the continued upkeep of the communal quarters.

1

2

1. Artist Lane Marinho is among a new wave of young creatives moving into the Lausanne 2. Residents Andres Schipani and Alejandra Mejia were keen to restore the modernist gem 3. La Borda is home to a multi-generational mix 4. Architects Carles Baiges (on left) and Pol Massoni also live in the block

parks. Under vaulted, undulating wooden structures, seniors and youngsters will meet to exchange stories. Wheelchair-bound residents can share pavement space with buggies, and young and old can nurture rooftop gardens side by side.

It sounds like a utopian vision yet given global demographic trends – the world's rapidly ageing population – this type of architecture shouldn't feel novel. Nor should it be the exception. In fact, it's a crucial response to the pressing, unrelenting reality that faces us.

Other spots for hanging up your hat in later years have been less engineered, with communities that engage well with the elderly forged in a more organic manner. **Mas de Tanit (4)** in Antibes in the South of France is a perfect example. The complex contains more than 700 flats spread between 15 blocks, each named after an old Phoenician port on the Mediterranean to commemorate Antibes' (or Antipolis's) history as a stopover for Phoenician traders. Names such as Carthage and Byblos are marked in bright-yellow lettering on burgundy signs and each building's entranceway also has its own colourful mosaic. A team of gardeners maintains three hectares of grounds, who tend to planters of hibiscus, petunias and plumbago, as well as pomegranate, olive and palm trees. "Mas de Tanit is like a little village. We have a night guard as well as a caretaker in the day," says resident Huong Gallois. "People live well here." An average day for residents involves a morning dip in the pool, a wander along the palm tree-lined boulevard leading to Antibes, perhaps followed by a café au lait by the beach or on their terrace before watching the sunset illuminate the umbrella pine trees.

The buildings are adorned with balconies shaded by orange awnings almost as sun-worn as the residents beneath them. Mas de Tanit, like much of the French Riviera, is a centre for leather-coloured tans that have been decades in the making – but there's a lively mix of nationalities settling here too. "The average age of residents is about 60," says Brigitte Calandri, who has been the building's caretaker since the late 1980s. "There are people from all over: Ireland, Italy, Germany, Sweden – and still a lot of French."

Older residents enjoy a tranquil life here and the scale of the site means there are always fresh faces coming and going, with families more than welcome. And in true Mediterranean style, the large turquoise pool at the centre of the complex closes at 13.00 and reopens at 15.00, meaning everyone's siestas remain undisturbed.

La Borda
Barcelona
La Borda is a great example of how co-housing can nourish a community. Built in timber – a material proven to improve wellbeing – the apartment block is designed to enhance the lives of all within. Communal areas allow older residents who live alone to spend time with young families while busy parents get a bit of extra help in caring for their children – a win-win situation.

3

4

Mas de Tanit
Antibes
Mas de Tanit might have begun as a holiday development in the 1960s but life here today is for many a more permanent affair. The older tenants who enjoy a full year on-site are greeted by the friendly faces of those who head to their second homes at the weekend. This mix of permanent and semi-permanent dwellers creates a vibrant energy and a holiday vibe whatever the season.

2

3

1

4

5

7

6

8

1. A communal pool sits at the heart of the complex 2. Huong and Bernard Gallois outside their penthouse apartment 3. Jonathan Philbois lives in Mas de Tanit 4. Christiane David, resident for 25 years 5. Local Jean-Pierre 6. Holiday-makers Vincent Greene and Nash Robb 7. Each building is named after an old Phoenician port 8. The sprawling site comprises over 700 apartments

1. Architecture firm Big designed 79&Park apartment block, in front of which residents gather for a friendly game 2. The building's central courtyard provides a place for neighbours to stop and chat

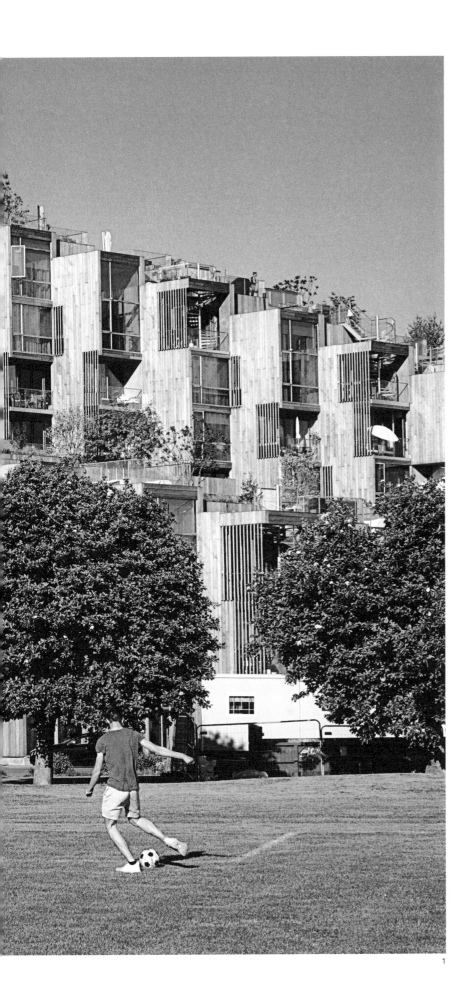

79&Park
Stockholm
Stockholm's cedar-wrapped apartment complex 79&Park sits on a verdant hill and uses its green space as a powerful tool to lure families from the sprawling suburbs into more compact living quarters. Shady planted areas higher up in the block create privacy for tenants, while the fact that they're living closer to the city and sharing facilities reduces the carbon footprint of their daily lives.

1

2

1

2

4

3

5 6

7

1. A café in art deco estate Tiong Bahru 2. A preschool outing at Skyville 3. The Skyterrace at Dawson was completed in 2015 4. Locals gather at Ghim Moh Market and Food Center 5. Bike sharing station 6. Skyville's verdant rooftop garden 7. Tanglin Halt is one of the oldest HBD estates in Singapore

HBD development
Singapore
In land-scarce Singapore citizens must make the most of what little they have, but lack of space has not stood in the way of quality of life – if anything, it has helped forge a unique sense of national pride and togetherness. Good design has played a key role, with communal buildings such as food halls, gardens and parks offering welcoming spaces for all.

Barbican Estate
London
Designed to cater to all lifestyles
and provide everything its tenants
could ever need, the Barbican
Estate offers gardens, lakes,
tennis and basketball courts,
secret passages, neighbourhood
organisations and more. The
estate's homes themselves come
in various sizes from studio flats
to four-bedroom houses.

1

1. The Barbican's lakes bring vital greenery and nature into the heart of the estate 2. The complex features a mix of private and public spaces

1

2

3

1. The sports centre brings residents together for activities like martial arts 2. Shared spaces are perfect for workouts 3. Greenery brightens the generous balconies 4. Older tenants enjoy a game of Tischtennis 5. Art class 6. Each building has a swimming pool and sauna at its top 7. A view over Wohnpark

4

Wohnpark Alt-Erlaa
Vienna
Sometimes a community
development can become
something of a micro-city and
Vienna's Alt-Erlaa project, which
houses roughly 10,000 people,
is an example of this in the best
possible way. Residents have
access to numerous community
clubs ranging from reading groups
to badminton meet-ups – sign us up
for the sun-bathing society please.

5

6

7

The neighbourhoods

Britz

Berlin, Germany

Berlin is known as the city of cool –
or so go the clichés. But beyond Mitte's
boutiques and cafés, Charlottenburg's
grand apartments and Neukölln's
vibrant multicultural bar mile lies a
neighbourhood called Britz. More quaint
than cool – instead of bars and boutiques
it's home to a warren of streets that winds
its way around rows of houses – here,
neighbours chat under their fruit trees
and might be overheard swapping a ladder
for a lawnmower.

In the centre of it all is a sweeping
three-storey building in the shape of a
horseshoe; its curving arms hugging
a central park. This not-really-suburban
place is a small oasis in the city and

(perhaps surprisingly) it is also an
architectural icon called the *Hufeisensiedlung*
("Horseshoe Estate"). Constructed between
1925 and 1930, it's a prime example of the
era in which Mitteleuropean cities like
Berlin erected large-scale social housing
projects to accommodate new city dwellers
with an eye to improving the lots of the
working and middle classes. Its architect
Bruno Taut was thinking theoretically but
for residents, then and now, the Horseshoe
Estate is simply a great place to live.

Around 7,000 people live here on about
29 hectares. It's a quietly busy place. And
despite the houses' seriality, the streets
and gardenscapes are visually varied,
with windows that pop in different accent

1   2

colours and building exteriors painted in an assortment of rich hues.

In its hey-day, the houses here were particularly sought-after but as the original residents aged and Berlin languished as a divided city, the Horseshoe Estate was somewhat forgotten. Only in the late 1990s and early 2000s did younger families rediscover the advantages of its charms when Berlin began selling off the properties. "Everyone who rented here was asked if they wanted to buy," says Ben Buschfeld, a longtime resident. "Buying wasn't always viable for 80-year-olds, so they left. New residents moved in – couples with one or two kids who wanted to be close to the city but also have a garden."

In 2007 Buschfeld and his wife Katrin Lesser founded a nonprofit to encourage residents to not only meet one another, but to learn more about the houses they live in (the Horseshoe is UNESCO-listed).

It's been nearly a century since its conception but the Estate feels increasingly contemporary. Buschfeld explains that conditions now are similar to those in the 1920s: a population influx, the appeal of compact living, sustainability and urban gardening. "If you show up here you might think at first that this is awful. But you look again and then you see a kind of village life in the metropolis," says resident Annette Birkholz, as she plucks an apple from her tree. "It's phenomenal."

1. Katrin Lesser and Ben Buschfeld at home 2. Architect Bruno Taut was famous for his colourwork 3. Checking up on the perennials
4. Inside the Horseshoe 5. Resident Constance Gesse in her kitchen 6. Bright, blocky balconies 7. Annette Birkholz in her front garden

The Sea Ranch
California, USA

1

About three hour's drive north of San Francisco is a community that stretches along miles of coastline where more than 2,000 houses nestle near cliffs or in the wooded forest. Built in the early 1960s by Oceanic Properties, a subsidiary of a Hawaiian property developer, The Sea Ranch is a product of its time, conceived with utopian ideals that emphasised the outdoors. Houses have a minimalist design aesthetic and remain modest in size.

Defined by a muted palette of greys and browns, the homes are predominantly clad in re-sawn tongue-and-groove redwood and, here and there, cedar shingle or plywood. Chad DeWitt, an architect who has lived here since 2017, owns a house

2

3

4

designed by Joseph Esherick, where an enamelled metal artwork by Barbara Stauffacher Solomon hangs in the kitchen. The graphic designer was instrumental in forging the community's visual identity, coming up with its ram's-head logo and the "supergraphics": a mixture of oversized fonts and geometric shapes seen in one of the communal swimming pools.

And the swimming pools aren't the only amenities residents can access: there are tennis, pickleball (a paddleball game), basketball and volleyball courts for those wanting a sunny run-around. There are also horse stables, 80km of hiking trails and a golf course. The Sea Ranch also has a community library and meeting rooms.

While the median Ranch dweller remains a retiree, a younger set has been re-establishing some of its lofty ideals. Among them is Leslie Redick, who has lived here since 2016. A fan of the community's landscape architect and planner Lawrence Halprin, she works for The Sea Ranch Association, which oversees regulations. She resides in a corner house in The Clusters, an area designed by William Turnbull. "I'm a relaxed person but I like rules," she says. "You can't live here if you don't – they keep the place beautiful."

It's this notion of a strictly preserved design aesthetic that either becomes cloying or vital, depending on which side of the fence you sit. The Association's

Department of Design, Compliance and Environmental Management regulates building fabrics, ensures exterior lighting is shielded and prohibits post-boxes outside homes. DeWitt jokes about the fact that all signage has a 30-degree angle on top and mentions the "Barnies": the stewards who closely guard what events take place at the communal Big White Barn. But for new arrivals, 1960s utopia still rings true.

At The Sea Ranch rules governing everything from materials to foliage create a strong aesthetic. The result here is one of the US's most attractive communities, with a look that has maintained the vision of its architects. It feels as fresh today as it did in the 1960s.

1. Residents having a sundowner 2. One of The Sea Ranch's three pools 3. Jeremy and Martin Otis 4. DeWitt's home, designed by Joseph Esherick 5. Jeremy Otis's extension to the couple's house 6. Heading to the beach 7. Megan Bellue and Monty Anderson 8. DeWitt's home looks out over woodland

Philopappou
Athens, Greece

There's no denying that more young Athenians are opting to live near the city centre than ever before, thanks to a renewed kick in the capital's cultural, culinary and business prospects. Philopappou neighbourhood, which is perched under the pine-covered hill of the same name, is where these new city dwellers are turning. "I've always loved how quiet and calm this small pocket of Athens is," says 30-year-old Alexia Stamatelatou, who moved to the area in 2020 with her partner, pharmacist Dimitris Karamitsos, and their dog Cosmo. While part of the Greek capital's charm is its bustle, this has also meant that finding calmer

1

2

3

and greener corners of this lively city has become a quest of its own.

Despite being a stone's throw from the Acropolis with its swathes of tourists, the winding footpaths of Philopappou hill and its sweeping views of Athens are a local's haven. "On weekends we buy fresh bread from Morning Bar, grab a coffee from Neratzia Cafe and then walk all the way around Philopappou Hill, bumping into friends and meeting new dogs," says Stamatelatou, who works in marketing. "You forget that you're in the centre of Athens!" She explains that her favourite views are the sea of lush cacti and flora-filled balconies, as well as the scattered rooftop pools. "I love all the neoclassical

houses in soft pastel colours, built climbing up the hill – each garage door is custom-made to accommodate the diagonal path of the road!"

The area is steeped in architectural history. Traditional townhouses stand next to modernist, minimalist and even surrealist structures. A case in point is the home of fêted Greek fashion designer Orsalia Parthenis, a renovated former-office building that was originally built in the 1970s. She shares the abode with her husband and two sons and explains that the design was inspired by the work of American architect John Lautner and the Maison de Verre in Paris. "People move at a slower pace in Philopappou," says

Parthenis. "My work life can get quite hectic, so it's great to live somewhere that's a counterbalance."

Philopappou's greatest feat, though, is instilling the sense of a small community among its residents, thanks largely to mainstays including the *laiki* (farmer's market). "I buy fresh produce each week from our *laiki* and walk away with far too many rare succulents and plants from the flower shop I Do," says Stamatelatou. "In minutes you can go to the Acropolis, shoot down towards the sea or go all the way up Philopappou Hill and enjoy views of the Saronic Gulf," says Karamitsos. "There's something special in the air around here, come and see for yourself!"

1. View from inside a *kafenion* (coffee house) 2. Tents lining the weekly *laiki* (farmer's market) on Kallidromiou street 3. Krokos house kitchen leading onto a courtyard 4. Leti Arvaniti-Krokou (top left) and family 5. Alekos Zannas at home 6. Picking lemons 7. Spiky shadows 8. Market day

Beaumaris

Melbourne, Australia

When residential development along Port Phillip Bay, south of Melbourne, took off in the 1950s, innovators such as Robin Boyd, David Chancellor and William Patrick all made their mark on the low-lying patch of coastal turf known as Beaumaris. Over time, it came to be seen as a place where the principles of modernist building met a distinctly Australian context.

Today, a brief stroll through the leafy streets reveals an abundance of well-considered homes along with flourishing parkland and shops. The residents, many of whom are designers and architects, form a tight-knit community: on Tuesday evenings, white haired locals play bowls in front of a clubhouse with a dramatically

1

2

3

sloping roof; a few streets away, the Beaumaris Art Group offers tutorials in a skylit brick studio built in 1965; at the weekend, the air is filled with the sound of children playing Australian rules football. Melbourne's skyline shimmers on the horizon but feels almost irrelevant.

Matt Skinner and his wife Carly arrived in the suburb after searching for a place where their children could enjoy what Carly describes as a "quintessentially Australian outdoor childhood". Beaumaris stood out not only for its community but the pristine coastline and clifftop walks, inviting cafés, reliable bus links and good schools. The couple were also taken with the area's rich architectural history – the

house they live in was designed in 1960 by Melbourne architect David Godsell.

Most of the suburb's postwar homes were designed to exist in harmony with the vegetation. Floor-to-ceiling windows and skylights in the Skinners' home connect the interior to the surrounding flora. "One of the things that attracted us to the house was how it is harmonious with the land," Matt says. The home of former photo stylist Alison Alexander is another typical example. Designed in the 1950s by Mockeridge, Stahle & Mitchell – which included Alexander's architect father Ross Stahle – its large windows allow light to filter in while framing the beauty of nearby foliage. The building's relatively small

footprint also helps it camouflage into the landscape. "It's not the largest house but it works beautifully," says Alexander. "I've never understood the people who think bigger homes are automatically better."

Residents such as Alexander and Matt are keen to preserve these smaller homes, which have become integral to the area's allure: "We're pushing the council to be stricter on conservation," says Annie Price, the vice president of Beaumaris Modern, an organisation dedicated to preserving the suburb's mid-century architecture. "This place just becomes more graceful with time," Matt says about his house. "Our job is to preserve it for the next person who lives here."

1. The Skinners' family home, Godsell House 2. Front façade of Godsell House 3. Matt and Carly Skinner 4. Annie Price, Jamie Paterson and their daughter Dottie 5. Cliffs along Port Phillip Bay 6. Residents are keen to conserve the area's prewar housing stock

4

5

6

Roccamare

Tuscany, Italy

The creation of Roccamare – southern Tuscany's secret modernist paradise – was no happy accident: it was the result of some very progressive and considered mid-century planning. In 1952, Count Federigo Ginori Conti bought this 200-hectare tranche of immaculate pine forest. Inspired by what he saw being created at Punta del Este in Uruguay, he set about developing Roccamare. Foremost in overseeing this delicate process was Florentine architect Ugo Miglietta, who drew up the division of the pinewoods into some 200 lots, each with a villa (most of which he also designed) set around gently meandering roads and paths with easy access to the pristine beach.

"I can only describe it as a sort of magic place," says the glamorous Genny Santini Gabellieri, who explains why, after her first visit at the age of 26, she was lured to life under the shade of the pines: "From that point I decided to live here with my family." A resident since the 1970s, she is one of the few year-round residents and is known affectionately as the Regina (queen) of Roccamare.

Another summertime resident, Valerie, Lady Solti, has been coming to her villa since 1965. "It was very different then," she says. "But I suppose the world was too." Back then only a few dozen of Roccamare's villas had been constructed and the village was somewhat of a wilderness; with no

1

2   3

shops, restaurants or streetlights even today, it is still very sparsely developed. It had, however, already attracted a gaggle of illustrious residents: "Well, James Bond used to bring us the British papers on his bike," says Lady Valerie, referring to long-time "Roccamarista" Roger Moore. "Luciano Pavarotti would often come too," she says. "He would make us spaghetti." Italian literary greats Italo Calvino and Carlo Fruttero were also regulars.

Despite the impressive roll call this place exudes little luxury – flat roofs and rusticated stone-wall finishes abound. In one spot a travertine slab projects out of a rock wall to form a bench and concrete awnings are perforated to

4

accommodate the trunks of the mighty umbrella pines whose canopy provides a beautifully dappled shade.

Roccamare's roads are unblemished by fences, gates or walls; a solitary sun-bleached sign warning of the risk of fire stands next to a rough hand-painted wooden plank denoting a lot number or family name. With each lot assigned its own straw-roofed *capanna* (beach hut) and shaded picnic table you'll find no plastic parasols or sun loungers here (also the result of an unspoken but widely acknowledged rejection of such objects). Gabellieri has a final thought on Roccamare: "People come here to disappear – it's liberating."

1. Villa Bartolini's current owners 2. Villa Settepassi by Pier Niccolò Berardi 3. Villa Baldassini 4. Roccamare beach 5. House of Genny Santini Gabellieri by Ugo Miglietta 6. The living room of Villa Bartolini by Ernesto Nathan Rogers 7. Villa Bartolini's exterior 8. Roccamare's trusty handyman in his Ape truck

5   6

7   8

Ari
Bangkok, Thailand

1

Descending from the Skytrain station, the sights, sounds and smells of Ari in Bangkok command attention from the street below. This neighbourhood is a raucous Siamese day-and-night affair. Everyone feasts and a festival-like cheer is rife. Durian fruits are split and snacked upon by businessmen and lush flowers for Buddhist offerings are sold into the early hours.

Yet peel away from this bustling intersection and you'll find a community pedalling along at a more leisurely pace. Ari is the leafy last bastion of mid-century suburban Bangkok, an area marked by a low-rise and tropical modern vernacular. With its 1950s and 1960s residences lolling

2

3

4

5

on large grassy blocks it's a far cry from the denser districts nearby.

"Here we have modernism in a tropical Thai way so you can see why we'd want to preserve it," says architect Chuta Sinthuphan, who likes to frequent Laliart Coffee, a café that adjoins his neighbourhood shop, Tokyobike. Despite the traffic, citizens love to cycle in Bangkok and particularly Ari, where there is less need to dexterously dodge tuk-tuks.

Ari is still one of the capital's most habitable quarters thanks to its longtime residents. Here the neighbourhood's condensed land ownership between wealthy and politically connected families remains potent. Many proud residents simply refuse to sell and as a collective they have the power to veto proposed developments. "The sense of community is strong in Ari," says Poi Drahmoune, a humanitarian aid worker who has lived in Ari since 2016. "Many of the places are small businesses, owned by people who are passionate about what they do."

Its laidback atmosphere, a rarity amid Bangkok's inherently frenetic energy, has led to a burgeoning scene of cafés, bars and restaurants as well as a number of independent retailers. In fact, each business has seemingly found its niche: The Yard hostel, constructed from shipping containers, hosts live music and movie nights in its leafy garden while in Phayathai Pirom park locals can peruse well-stocked shelves at an open-air library set beneath the towering Skytrain tracks. Elsewhere, specialist coffee shops sit moments from local vendors who have been trading in the community for decades.

"Ari is a Thai family neighbourhood," says Aurapraphan Sudhinaraset, who is the managing director of fashion label Vickteerut. "It's a small community, which fits with our vision to mix nature and traditional culture with the city. I think success is defined differently here. If I am happy and if my colleagues and customers are happy, then that is enough for me."

1. View of Ari 2. Father and son meet for a tennis match 3. A sunny spot in Chuta Sinthuphan's home 4. Locals at a swing dance class 5. Running track
6. The Gump community mall 7. Coffee at Camp Cafe 8. Furry friends at the Dog In Town Cafe 9. Inside The Yard hostel 10. The Yard hostel's garden

6

7

10

8 9

Greenery
Put down some roots

Good for wellbeing and transformative in the home, gardening is the perfect foil to modern life – whether in the form of a simple houseplant, Zen garden or rooftop bursting with vegetables. It's time to get your hands dirty.

For most of their history cities have looked to clear wild spaces and tame nature, but we're luckily rediscovering the value of letting it back in – whether that's promoting a breeze (rather than cranking up the air-con) or bringing the calming properties of plants into the home. From the simple, hopeful lemon tree gently tended over winter to the fully-fledged vegetable patch, making space for flowers and plants and giving them our care and attention makes us feel better. Urban greenery between homes and in gardens can also store water, soak up carbon and help biodiversity – in large numbers plants and trees can even lower the ambient temperature of our cities. A little foliage can go a long way and this chapter celebrates the virtue of dirt under your fingernails.

We take a look at the traditional garden and learn how tending one can enhance our wellbeing and provide creative inspiration. Next, we task a few cultivated souls with offering insight on the benefits of the humble houseplant. Getting a touch more adventurous we seek the wisdom of a landscape architect and consider how greenery can be woven into the designs

of our residential buildings and the spaces between them in a way that's beautiful.

Alongside advice we serve up some visual inspiration from Milan's rooftop gardens to sunny plant-laden patios in Brazil and even a beautiful Belgian home. Go on, branch out.

1
2

3
4

A patch of green
Growing gains

Studies have shown gardening to be as effective as therapy when treating stress disorders. It's not hard to see why; aside from the perfect combination of fresh air, direct sunlight and physical exercise, cultivating our own greenery (no matter how little the plot) is a way to reconnect with the natural world. It's time spent away from screens and the hectic distractions of modern life.

In many ways, tending a garden can be a great leveller. Unlike painting, gardening doesn't require much natural talent. It's not as expensive as training to ski or scuba dive, nor does it require as much equipment or demand as much physical ability. Unlike learning to play an instrument, you don't have to sit practising for hours on end. It's beautifully simple; all you need is water, sunlight, a few seeds and a patch of dirt – along with a willingness to get some of it under your fingernails.

Gardens can be places of inspiration and sanctuary right on your doorstep – literally. From Christian Dior to Derek Jarman, the greatest creative minds are often linked by a love of gardening. Monet went so far as to describe his garden as his "greatest masterpiece". In fact, it was as much a means of self-expression as his paintings: he filled the land surrounding his house in the French village of Giverny with densely planted flowerbeds arranged in blocks of colour that changed throughout the seasons. It was a technicolour world with sections of bright red geraniums, deep purple irises and yellow, pink and red roses.

But with over 50 per cent of the world's population living in urban areas, a big, leafy garden is something of a luxury for many. A green home, however, isn't solely the reserve of those with plenty of outdoor space. City-dwellers have long sought pleasure in cultivating greenery in every available nook; from window boxes to balconies and pots around the house.

5

In 2019, Souad Abdallah began planting seeds on the rooftop of her home in the Beirut neighbourhood of Furn Al-Shebbek. "Beirut lacks a lot of public spaces and greenery," says Abdallah, "I thought if living here means I don't have access to nature, I'll just bring nature to me." This was during a time of great political unrest in the city and, when she saw how enthusiastically her neighbours offered to help tend her patch, Abdallah realised the potential her garden had to bring people together. She decided to launch her own grassroots initiative to unite the local community around gardening. The result is Kon, a collective which runs horticultural workshops and helps others set up permaculture gardens in their homes in Furn Al-Shebbek. "It's a solidarity movement," says Abdallah, "I felt the urge to show how we needed to work together despite our differences."

Today, Souad's rooftop is an oasis bursting with kale, lettuce and chard. "Growing vegetables in an urban space can be challenging," says Abdallah, "but it's so rewarding. One seed produces many seeds. It's wonderful how generous nature is. I recommend everyone grows plants even if you only have a small corner. It's like meditation, it relaxes the brain."

Houseplants are also an important means of bringing greenery inside. Not only do they improve indoor air quality by producing oxygen, they're prized for their aesthetic qualities. "I see plants as a kind of sculpture," says Magali Elali, Antwerp-based co-author of *Greenterior*, a book that delves into the homes of green-fingered creatives. "In our place, we've positioned the furniture according to the plants and not the other way around." The significance of getting the spot right is something Elali believes is often underestimated by budding plant parents. "People go crazy when it comes to watering but that's not the most important part," says Elali. "Do your research and find out which conditions suit your greenery best. Most need to be somewhere warm where they'll receive plenty of sunlight."

Recent years might have seen a boom in houseplants but the height of their popularity was perhaps in Victorian-era Britain. Advancements in architecture meant warmer homes with more natural light, providing the climate for hardy houseplants. In the late 19th century no well-appointed British home was complete without an array of ferns, palms and the odd potted citrus tree. Keen greenhouse builders, they cultivated exotic specimens brought back by intrepid "plant hunters".

1. Apple picking in Ontario 2. Milanese architecture firm Piuarch's vegetable patch 3. The exterior of Viewpoint, a Tucson home designed by Judith Chafee 4. Picking fresh herbs in Carcassonne 5. At a community garden in Valencia

1. The green courtyard of Casa CSF in São Paulo was designed in the 1940s 2. A shady terrace in Los Angeles 3. Potted olive trees adorn a Milanese roof terrace 4. Magali Elali and son Nolan tend to their houseplants 5. A flower-filled balcony in Beirut

1

2

3

5

4

2

1

3

These botanical adventurers travelled the world to track down rare trees and flowers and their bounty became highly coveted status symbols among well-to-do aesthetes. Royal lilies, for example, were introduced to Europe by Ernest Wilson in 1903. He encountered the flowers growing in China's Min Valley and nearly died in a landslide while collecting them.

These prized plants, which explorers like Wilson risked life and limb to find, are now so readily available that their roots are all but forgotten. Switzerland's beloved geraniums, for example, are native to South Africa and were brought to Europe in the 17th century. Today, 85 million of these brightly flowering plants are purchased by Swiss households each year but the obsession isn't necessarily a healthy one. "They may be beautiful," says Erwin Meier-Honegger, who runs Swiss garden centre Ernst Meier AG, "but being from South Africa means they're no good for biodiversity because our local insects can't eat them. If people insist on planting them, I tell them to put some native plants beside and not to be too precious about having their leaves nibbled by caterpillars. If the caterpillars had nothing to feed on, we'd have no butterflies and the whole local ecosystem would suffer."

The Victorians might have been particularly obsessed with the idea of importing plants from far-flung corners of the globe but it's a tradition that stretches far further back. "The Egyptians used to transport cut flowers to Rome," says Christopher Woodward, director of London's Garden Museum. The Victorians were, however, to thank for many of the most important innovations in outdoor equipment. "The garden hose was only invented in the 19th century," says Woodward, "and the lawnmower arrived in the 1830s. People would have previously had to use sheep to maintain their lawns." Despite all the tools and equipment we now have to keep our plots in check, Woodward notes how the best landscape designers still put great emphasis on letting nature take its course. "Gardening requires you to accept some kind of loss of control," he says. "Architecture, by contrast, is completely about control. For an architect, a building is at its best on day one and then it's downhill from there. The bronze tarnishes, the glass gets dirty. Whereas with a garden, it's only just the beginning."

The idea of harmony between garden and gardener is an important part of traditional Japanese landscape design. The country's oldest spaces were created in line with indigenous Shinto beliefs, according to which everything from waterfalls to rocks and trees are inhabited by *kami* (spirit gods) rendering them sacred. The focus, therefore, was not on the taming of plants but creating a sense of peaceful balance with them. The arrival of Buddhism cemented the idea of it as a meditative sanctuary and Zen gardens sprung up around Buddhist monasteries. These were miniaturised versions of Japan's landscape where a rock became a mountain, a pond an ocean and exquisitely pruned bonsai trees symbolised an entire forest. "I believe the Japanese approach of persuading and stimulating nature will have a greater future value than the predominant Western method of conquering and exploiting her," noted Bauhaus-founder Walter Gropius following a visit in 1955.

A contemporary update of this can be found in gallerist Taka Ishii's Tokyo home. Designed by architect Akihisa Hirata in 2017, the structure comprises concrete boxes slotted together and interwoven with small terraces and balcony gardens that jut out from the building's exterior. The formation of the house is inspired by that of a tree, with a trunk at its centre and small pockets of greenery weaving their way upwards like branches. Over a hundred varieties of plants fill its modular terraces, including pomegranate trees and blueberry bushes and a range of flowers chosen to bloom at different points of the year so the house never loses its colour. According to Ishii, there's only one nod to Japanese gardening traditions: "If you build a house in Japan, you have to plant a tree for good luck. So we have one on the terrace right at the top of the building."

For Auckland-based landscape designer Xanthe White, weaving greenery into the fabric of a building is something she is seeing more of her clients move towards. "People don't always want the garden to be the decoration around the box," she says. "A house can be spread across a site, which allows the landscape to really breathe through it." According to White, her clients are increasingly recognising the benefits of bringing nature closer to their lives. "People really value green and its calmness," she says. "Waking up and looking at trees definitely changes your brain. So does being connected to the way the seasons change. What I love most about gardening is the anticipation. My husband will wait attentively for the magnolias to bloom because it signals that the coldest part of winter is over."

When plotting designs, White puts great emphasis on matching the garden to the gardener. "The skill of a designer is not imposing an ideal on someone but instead seducing them into action," says White, who invests time ensuring her clients feel fully equipped with the horticultural know-how to keep their gardens looking sharp. "You need to listen and get a sense of a person before you start. It's important the design matches their personality and ability," says White. "You can make a beautiful dress but if you put it on someone who doesn't feel comfortable wearing it, it's not going to work."

4

1. Climbers cover a Milanese balcony 2. Lena Mahr and her son at their Berlin home 3. Ben Shaw's permaculture garden in Geelong, Australia
4. Souad Abdallah and neighbours in Beirut

1

1. Valencia's brutalist residential complex Espai Verd 2. A balcony shaded by palm trees in Merano 3. Paved terrace at the Villa St Martin in Alsace
4. A stone path lined with tropical plants at Casa CSF in São Paulo

2

3   4

1. Walkway at Tucson's Levin Residence 2. Greenery outside Viewpoint 3. A shaded coffee spot in Long Beach, California 4. Bonsai is thought to have arrived in Japan from China centuries ago 5. Casa CSF's original windows 6. The Baker family's farmhouse in Ontario 7. John Pylypczak's Toronto garden

1 2

3 4

5

6   7

1. Cascading balconies brimming with foliage and flowers in Valencia 2. Light pours into The Clock Building in California 3. Designer John Pylypczak
4. Pockets of greenery in Beirut

1

2

3   4

Materials
Solid foundations

We are living in a material world – architects today have countless options when it comes to construction. We review six classic materials and conclude that natural is always better.

Materials matter. The walls that surround and protect us also influence how we feel. This chapter scratches the surface of a rather physical matter and offers a simple run-down of the best mediums to build with and the properties that can enhance your everyday life.

Unsurprisingly, many of the canniest answers come from the world around us rather than man-made alternatives. We've made homes from wood since the dawn of domestic life and today it remains a hardy and flexible answer to contemporary buildings (it smells good too). Thanks to a dash of modern know-how and new construction techniques, wood is having a renaissance in residential design.

Beyond that there is the glass that lets light into our living spaces and the stone floors helping to keep humid homes cool underfoot. Concrete isn't the panacea that many hoped for in the 1960s and 1970s but there are lessons to learn here from its versatility and hardiness that are as relevant now as ever.

From humble dwellings to regal residences, we showcase the way in which wise material choices can create homes that touch us.

A construction classic for a reason, this natural number is as beautiful as it is hardy.

Wood

Timber is the age-old building material that never dates and in recent years its use has enjoyed a huge resurgence in the building industry, with new technologies allowing wooden apartment blocks to soar to the sky. But the natural properties of wood have always made homes more idyllic places to live in – spend a few nights enjoying the alpine hues of a Swiss timber chalet or dipping into a Hinoki tub and delighting in the aroma that's generated and you'll catch our drift. If all this still hasn't convinced you that timber's raw beauty can be uplifting and restorative, then we urge you to pay a visit to the student dormitory of Copenhagen's 4th May College (*pictured, above*). Designed by architect Hans Hansen in the late 1940s, and lovingly restored by Bertelsen & Scheving Arkitekter, its mahogany-panelled walls, ceilings and balustrades create a warm and cosy environment for residents to retreat to.

Liljestrand House
Hawaii
On the outskirts of Honolulu,
the timber balustrade and cladding
of this property by Vladimir Ossipoff
riffs on its forested location.

Strandparken
Sweden
Designed by Wingårdh Arkitektkontor,
residents here say they breathe easier
in their apartments, which smell like
freshly chopped wood.

The Landscape Lodge
France
The timber frame of this traditional
chalet blends it into the surrounds;
it's complemented by a soft palette
of natural materials inside.

Zürich residence
Switzerland
The Japanese design smarts of Yuichi
Kodai combine with high-end Swiss
carpentry to transform an old Zürich
apartment into a heavenly new abode.

Kjaerholm residence
Denmark
Wooden walls and seaweed floors
in the home of celebrated Danish
minimalist Poul Kjaerholm; all
exposed timber has been left untreated.

Perhaps the most contemporary of all,
this material makes light work of building.

Glass

Big, blocky towers of glass are often considered eyesores but when this material is applied correctly to domestic settings the results can be life-enhancing. Famously, Mies van der Rohe's 1951 Illinois Farnsworth House – a glass box of a home – showcased how a house could be constructed in a manner that would allow plenty of natural light in, while also offering warmth and liveability for those dwelling there. Drawing upon new engineering techniques, Van der Rohe and the modernist designers of the period used glass to revitalise our idea of the contemporary home – and we are still enjoying the benefits today. A fine example can be found in the sun-soaked neighbourhood of Jardins, São Paulo (*pictured, above*). Here, a Zenon Lotufo-designed home – conceived in the 1940s – opens up to lush gardens thanks to windows and panelled doors that play with transparency and finishes, providing residents with a direct connection to the outdoors.

Killingsworth House
USA
Architect Ed Killingsworth's home in Long Beach, California, uses double-height ceilings and windows to blur the lines between indoors and out.

Bretagne Building
Brazil
Frosted glass windows in the dedicated "party room" of this São Paulo apartment building ensures there's natural light, and privacy, for those looking to cut loose.

Miller House
USA
This famed modernist home in Columbus, Indiana, uses extensive windows to seamlessly merge the interior and the garden.

Villa E
Morocco
Studio KO employed pivoting glass doors to maximise the views of the Atlas Mountains, grounding the property with a sense of place.

Bremen Cube
Germany
Translucent panels are part of the prefabricated kit designed by Berlin and Paris-based architects Lin for infill housing in Bremen.

An earthy option that's robust, readily available and comes in a variety of finishes.

Stone

Prized for its hardiness, stone has been used to create durable homes for millennia thanks to its ability to stand up to the scuffs of daily life, regulate temperature and resist damage caused by rot and mould. But it's more than just these practical features that make it so appealing. Its rustic – or sometimes polished – good looks have made it beloved by homemakers while its earthy quality allows designers to ground abodes in their surrounds; when used externally, stone can embed a structure within a landscape and make buildings appear as if they are literally rising from the earth. Architect Judith Chafee's work in the US is a case in point. The living area of her Rieveschl Residence in the foothills of the Coronado mountains (*pictured, above*) features stacked-stone walls, a hearth and built-in seating nook – all made from rock which was gathered on site, truly integrating the home with its setting.

Wallington homestead
Australia
Limestone walls and floors make this Clare Cousins-designed home appear as if it had emerged fully-formed from the landscape.

Seidler House
Australia
Locally quarried blue metal basalt in modernist master Harry Seidler's Sydney house imbues the space with a strong sense of place.

Baabdat home
Lebanon
Architect Joseph Yammine used limestone sourced on site to lend this home a weathered appearance to complement the rocky landscape.

Villa E
Morocco
Stone's hardiness means it can be used indoors and out, allowing the interior and exterior spaces to flow into each other.

Gold Coast residence
Australia
No two pieces of natural stone are the same making it possible to play with colour and texture, as seen in interior designer Janelle Watson-Evans' abode.

Puntaldia residence
Italy
One of 700 residences designed by Milanese architect Gianni Gamondi, this Sardinian villa positively glows in its local pink and white stone.

This material is simple, versatile and ubiquitous – where would we be without it?

Brick

There are several reasons why the humble brick has been the building block of choice for thousands of years: it's hard-wearing, easily maintained and often looks better with age. Made by mixing clay, sand and water before being kiln baked or air dried, it picks up points for sustainability and its knack for enhancing a home's sense of place when the material it draws upon is sourced locally. The brick's true strength, however, lies in its diminutive size – it can help grand homes feel intimate, and small homes cosy and warm. Its modular nature also allows flexibility to those who want to create sculptural, patterned or textured walls. For proof, look to architect Nguyen Hai Long's Termitary House in Da Nang, Vietnam (*pictured, above*), which brings all of these traits together. Using the area's baked bricks to create a lattice-like exterior wall, it is at once contemporary and a throwback to the brick-built Champa-era temples that have been standing in Vietnam for 1,000 years.

Park Towers
Colombia
Architect Rogelio Salmona's three-building development in Bogotá uses the modularity of bricks to play with different forms, heights and shapes.

Beacon Hill residence
USA
Brick buildings weather well – this red-brick converted stable in Boston is more than 100 years old yet still looks as good as new.

Muckle Flugga House
Australia
Bricks can add a playful, decorative element to a property, as seen in this imposing fireplace found in a suburb of Melbourne.

Birtcher-Share House
USA
Modernist designer Harwell Hamilton Harris' creation in Los Angeles uses bricks inside and out fusing the home in the landscape.

Though its heyday was enjoyed in the 1960s,
this man-made matter still has plenty to offer.

Concrete

Concrete is the most commonly used man-made building material on earth, thanks to the fact that it can be easily crafted into almost any shape imaginable. Take the official digs of the Swiss ambassador to Australia (*pictured, above*). This Canberra residence was designed by Hermann and Hans Peter Baur and features an elegant cantilevered concrete awning that curves over the front door – a welcoming gesture that beckons guests inside. And while the Baurs opted for an off-form surface, showing the contours of the timber moulds in a traditional shade of grey, the finishes and colour options for concrete are almost endless. Pigments can be added to give warmth, different stones can be used as an aggregate and the final surface can be polished for refinement or left raw for a more honest feel. All of this turns the narrative that concrete buildings are cold and soulless on its head; in reality they can be imaginative, colourful and cosy – and can make the perfect home.

Love2 House
Japan
This home makes use of concrete's versatility, creating bespoke forms to maximise space and light on a small lot in Tokyo.

Secular Retreat
UK
Swiss architect Peter Zumthor's design features rammed concrete with a dusty pigmentation that reflects the surrounding fields and landscape.

House in Sri Lanka
Sri Lanka
The exposed surfaces and angular concrete walls of revered Japanese architect Tadao Ando's design create a raw gallery-like aesthetic.

V4 House
Brazil
Architect Marcio Kogan's use of concrete, where no finish was added after timber formwork was removed, adds warmth to this minimalist house.

Casa Möbius
Mexico
The endless flexibility of concrete made the triangular hollows on the ceiling of architect Ernesto Gómez Gallardo Argüelles's home possible.

Bend it, fold it, coat it – metal is an almost endlessly malleable option.

Metal

The use of metal in the construction of residential projects owes a lot to the industrial manufacturing processes of the 20th century. While these paved the way for its use as an integral structural element, metal really shines when it's used as a surface – whether as exterior cladding or on interior worktops and ceilings. This flexibility – to be used indoors and out – is largely thanks to its range of finishes, forms and means of fixing: steel, copper, aluminium and zinc can be folded, stamped and coated in countless ways. Observe the anodised aluminium exterior of Küsnacht apartments, near Zürich (*pictured, above*). Designed by architect Mike Guyer, corrugated, semi-permeable sheets are used to clad nearly every inch of the apartment block, allowing a cross breeze, while also diffusing light and reflecting the colours of the neighbourhood's trees. It is this versatility in application and finish that means metal can be well-suited to a home in any climate and environment.

The Silo
Denmark
This Copenhagen apartment conversion by architecture firm Cobe has an angular façade that celebrates metal's striking natural finish.

Erhardtstrasse
Germany
Metal's malleability was leveraged by Munich-based Euroboden to create a custom woven ceiling effect that blends with the cobble paving below.

Spalding Hall
Hawaii
This building in Honolulu has a gold-colored metal mesh to protect windows from harsh afternoon sun, while still allowing airflow.

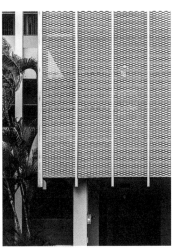

Zürich residence
Switzerland
Metal's structural possibilities and aesthetic beauty are on show in the columns and balustrades of this Swiss apartment building.

Weekend House Nové Hamry
Czech Republic
Architect David Zámecník used a darkened aluminium to reflect the shades of grey found in the nearby granite, basalt and tree trunks.

Details
Pay attention

We believe that inspiration can be found in the most unlikely of places. This is our personal scrapbook of the homely details that have caught our eye over the years – from Moroccan doorways to Spanish suntraps. Let's take a closer look.

Now we've shown you around, it is high time we zoomed in on the details. Small architectural touches can have a big impact and additions from the occupants are what make our dwellings distinct. This chapter provides a visual feast of finely-honed features to admire, many snapped on the road by MONOCLE's own photographers and editors. Some were captured in our neighbourhoods or the homes of friends, others were spotted on the streets of the cities and towns we've reported from. All are moments when we were drawn to these details for their character and appeal.

This is a journey into unseen homes that will hopefully spark some curiosity and offer inspiration and flair for your own space. There's an important nod to individuality – no two homes are or should be the same. It's also good to remember that ideas can come from anywhere, a glimpse through a window, a tactile door knob or knocker or a well-deployed bench.

From inviting doorways to impressive façades and stylish seating to luscious gardens we'll get you up close and personal with the details that turn the everyday into the extraordinary.

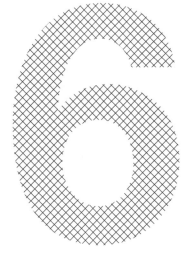

Façades

First impressions
On the face of it

We know you shouldn't judge a book by its cover, but a home's frontage is a sign of what's to come: a plant-dripping balcony, playful brickwork pattern or decorative iron grill can make all the difference.

Doors

Warm welcome
Enter here

More than a simple thoroughfare,
the threshold is an opportunity to
express oneself. And if that just so
happens to include a preposterous
lion-shaped door-knocker, so be it.

Plants

Go green
Bring the outdoors in

Whether a delicate maidenhair fern, easy-care cactus or the fanned-out fronds of a fiddle-leaf fig, the humble houseplant instantly changes the feel of a room. More is more when it comes to greenery.

Details

Gardens

Drinking and dining

Be our guest
Table manners

A rustic chopping board, mismatched crockery, a crumpled linen tablecloth and friends gathered around a table: it's the little things that make mealtimes special.

Space to grow
Flower power

As with any room, a garden requires a bit of furnishing: fill it with pockets of greenery or dot with pots bursting with blooms, but whatever you do, make sure there is a sun-drenched corner from which to enjoy all your hard work.

Fittings

Furniture

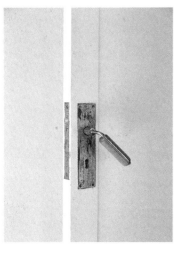

Finishing touches
The devil is in the details

Just because an item is functional
doesn't mean it can't be beautiful –
that one-of-a-kind door handle from
the flea market, bespoke curtain
pulley or antique coat hook will give
you pleasure every time you use it.

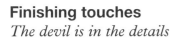

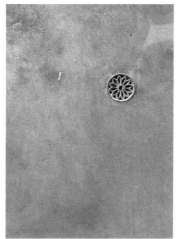

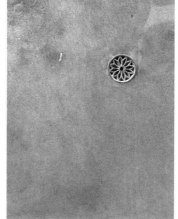

Fancy furnishings
Sitting pretty

A perfectly-proportioned stool, a handsome sideboard, that deep armchair that's calling to be sunk into: our homes are nothing without the pieces of furniture we fill them with.

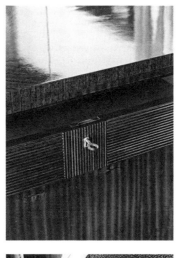

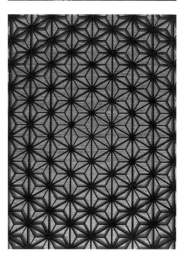

Indoor lighting

Glow your own way
The highlights

Lighting can instantly change the feel
of a space – for better or for worse.
We like to keep it soft, low and subtle
for a glow that you can relax into.

Natural lighting

Let the sunshine in
Illuminating stuff

Everything looks better when bathed
in sunlight – it's as simple as that.
There are few greater pleasures
than watching diffused and dappled
shadows play across the walls of your
own home.

Shelving

On display
A welcome sight

Colour-coded, mismatched,
minimalist – whatever your style,
shelves are a talking-point waiting
to happen. Rotate your curations
to keep things interesting.

Art

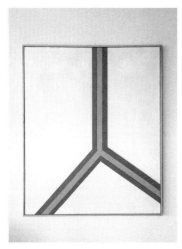

Pets

Creature comforts
In the dog house

Often found dozing in the best sun-
drenched corners or sprawled on
the comfiest armchair, pets are
arguably the true owners of the
home. And don't they know it.

Still life
Home is where the art is

The pieces that grace the walls and
surfaces of our homes are a true
reflection of the lives lived there.
These are the inimitable touches that
make a home unique.

Designs for living
Try this at home

Furnishing a house can be a daunting task – where to begin? We favour the slower approach, collecting pieces over time that make you feel something. But everyone has to start somewhere, so we've collated our favourite design items from around the world to kick you off. Just keep them to yourself.

This book is a celebration of the home but what about the act of furnishing one? Here we chart 100 failsafe items from sofas to cutting boards and lights to shelving units. Rest assured our decade-plus of perusing tradeshows, ateliers and design studios means that we've examined each one up close.

So what is a "design for living" exactly? Well, how our homes look is important but so too is the balance of practicality, longevity and provenance. Some of these products were designed decades ago and have stood the test of time but there are newer items in the mix and well-made creations from companies big and small. Larger retailers such as Muji and Ikea are successful for a reason – they have championed the usefulness of products in homes across the world – and they sit on our list alongside brands operating at the high-end of the furniture market as well as the small, honest and interesting producers.

Of course, there are a couple of indulgences too: the Italian-made Charlotte Perriand chaise longue won't be for everyone who buys this book but it made our rundown thanks to its uncompromising design and durability.

Our feeling? A house isn't defined by the presence of expensive design icons but if you're *going* to invest then why not buy the best you can, eh? So whether you plump for an affordable everyday item from a big-name brand or a one-off classic for the ages, we're confident that everything on our list can help you make your house a home.

1 Emma companion set
Eldvarm, Sweden

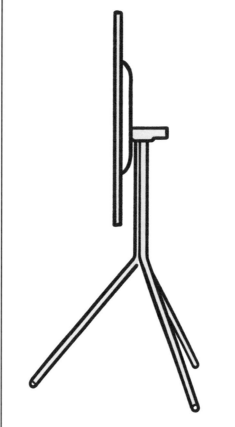

2 Nolita 5453T table
Pedrali, Italy

Made from steel in colours ranging from a classic white to a warm terracotta, this fold-down outdoor table is easy on the eye and enduring in style.

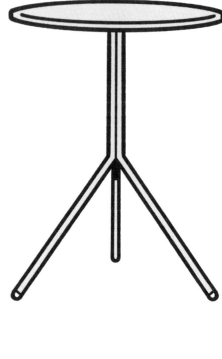

3 Formosa wall calendar
Danese Milano, Italy

4 Bamboo basket with handle
Native & Co, Japan

Organise your home with these fine and flexible bamboo baskets handwoven in Japan. Whether they're used to store fruit and veg or help keep your bathroom looking tidy, these containers will complement any room.

These smart, practical tools provide everything you need to stoke your fire on a winter evening while making a handsome accompaniment to your living room year round.

With removable PVC sheets, this perpetual wall calendar conceived by Enzo Mari in the 1960s draws on the best qualities of Italian design. Counting down the days never looked so good.

5 Nolita 3659 lounge chair
Pedrali, Italy

Another piece by Pedrali, this chair pays homage to Italian design maestro Mario Pedrali's first metal garden chair, created in 1963. The 2015 update is a sunny number for an even sunnier patio.

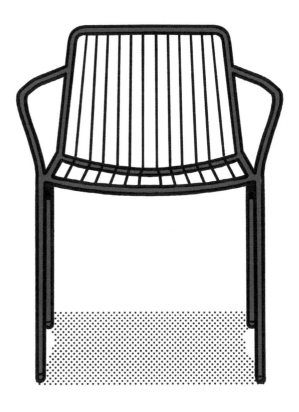

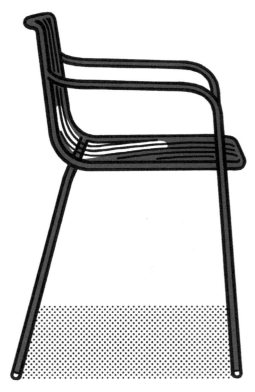

6 G-type soy sauce dispenser
Hakusan, Japan

A staple in Japanese homes since 1958, this porcelain soy sauce dispenser is fired at 1,300C. The easy-pour product is now found all over the world.

7 Stackable glass set
Muji, Japan

Clever pieces at an affordable price has long been the hallmark of Muji products and these stackable glasses symbolise the firm's mindset in the most elegant manner.

8 Vipp15 pedal bin
Vipp, Denmark

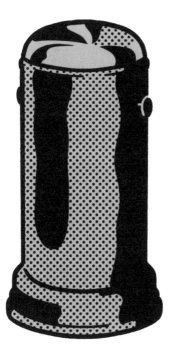

Many companies might shun the idea of a bin living at the heart of its identity but the Vipp15 pedal bin, which made the ordinary extraordinary in 1939, remains a brand bestseller to this day.

9
Modell III workshop stool
Girsberger, Switzerland

The height-adjustable Modell 111 stool was created in 1910 and the simple mechanism that alters the seat's level hasn't needed much updating since.

10
Armchair 311
Svenskt Tenn, Sweden

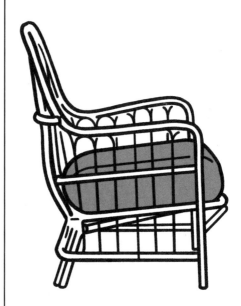

Josef Frank's 1930s number is a welcome addition to a lounge or sunroom. Made with light rattan, its presence immediately puts people at ease – and that's before they even sit on it.

11
Butterfly stool
Tendo Mokko, Japan

Japanese designer Sori Yanagi's famous stool consists of two symmetrical pieces of moulded wood joined with a brass fitting. Its timeless nature makes it feel at home with most interior styles.

12
CH37 dining chair
Carl Hansen & Søn, Denmark

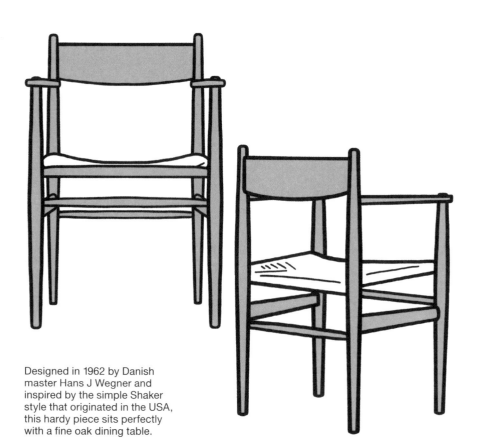

Designed in 1962 by Danish master Hans J Wegner and inspired by the simple Shaker style that originated in the USA, this hardy piece sits perfectly with a fine oak dining table.

13
Salt and pepper mills
Very Good & Proper, UK

Made from European beech by British company Very Good & Proper, these salt and pepper grinders are handsome enough to be kept on view long after the plates have been cleared.

14 Drop umbrella stand
Ishinomaki Laboratory, Japan

Rainy days aren't so bad when your umbrella stand unleashes the aromatic scent of western red cedar into the home. The Drop also stores up to nine umbrellas in a tidy, compact manner.

15 ST-350 two-tier toolbox
Fabrikat Working Goods, Switzerland

This well-ordered, two-level toolbox is bent from a only two sheets of steel making it extremely mobile and lightweight despite its volume. Made in Switzerland, it won't let you down.

16 Circular counter stool
Bassamfellows, USA

With a look that would be well-suited to a smoky 1960s whiskey saloon, the leather-lined cushion and plated-steel-tubing base make Bassamfellows' stool a must-have for any home bar.

17 522 Tokyo chaise longue
Cassina, Italy

A Charlotte Perriand classic, this refined recliner marries good aesthetics with body-contouring ergonomics. The 12 curved strips of wood are joined with satin-finished brass studs.

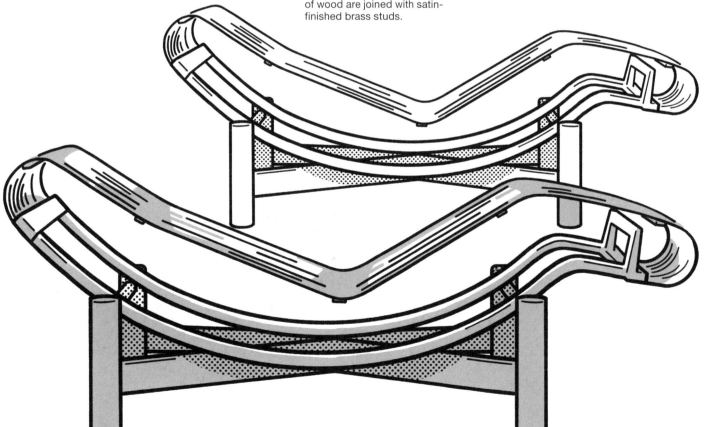

18 Formwork desk organiser
Herman Miller, USA

Conceived by London studio Industrial Facility, this charming modular organiser comes in a high-quality plastic and can be scaled up or down in size depending on how disorderly your desk is.

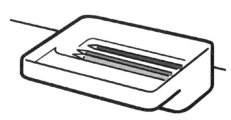

20 Pruning scissors
Labour and Wait, UK

For tough cutting, reach for the specially-shaped blades and extra long handles of these pruning scissors. Reliable and robust, they succeed in looking smart without sacrificing on performance.

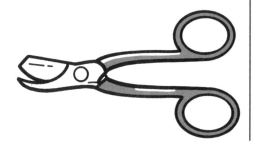

19 Mokuji planter cover
Araheam, Japan

Made in Japan from white oak and rattan, this plant pot holder provides an elegant way of showcasing your home's fledgling greenery, encasing your plants in the most natural of materials.

21 Lounge chair
Richard Lampert, Germany

German architect Herbert Hirche made this chair for his own house in 1953. Its minimalist, tubular-steel structure is inspired by the Bauhaus where Hirche studied under Mies van der Rohe in the early 1930s.

22 Cross chair
Takt, Denmark

Like all of Takt's furniture, this stackable wooden chair is delivered in flat-pack form. It's the work of London duo Pearson Lloyd and won the German Design Award in 2021.

23 Kevi 2533 swivel chair
Engelbrechts, Denmark

When architect Jørgen Rasmussen was commissioned to create a home for furniture manufacturer Bent Harlang in 1958, he was also asked to produce a chair to match the building – this was the result.

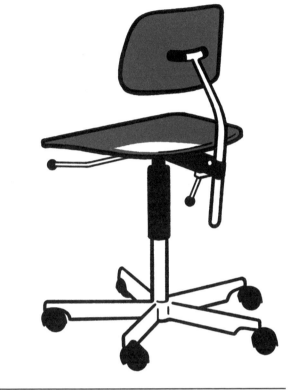

25 Planner magazine holder
Fritz Hansen, Denmark

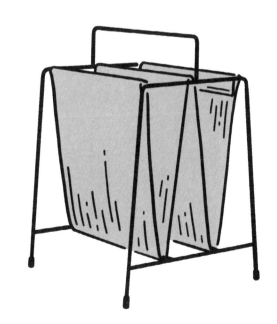

Paul McCobb devised this steel-framed magazine holder as part of his Planner series in the 1950s. A self-taught designer, McCobb revitalised interiors with his functional interpretations of classic forms.

24 Nurture water jug
Skultuna, Sweden

British designer Ilse Crawford is behind this sophisticated brass jug produced by Swedish foundry Skultuna, which was established in 1607 by King Karl IX.

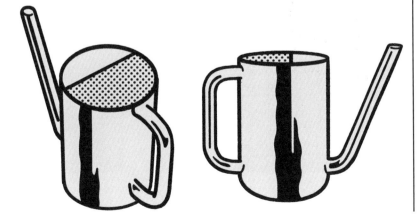

26 NychairX
NychairX, Japan

Takeshi Nii created this foldable design in 1970. Its removable seat is constructed from highly durable Kurashiki sailcloth and thanks to its lightweight frame, it comes in at a mere 6.5kg.

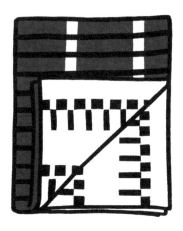

27 Dovetail blanket
Eleanor Pritchard, UK

Taking its name from the corner joints traditionally used in cabinet-making, Eleanor Pritchard's cosy geometric Dovetail blanket is made by a family-run woollen mill in Lancashire.

28 Stool 60
Artek, Finland

Alvar Aalto's simple stool is made entirely from Finnish birch. It was first produced in 1933 using Aalto's signature "L-leg" wood bending technique which he developed and patented himself.

29 Stoneware mug
Moheim, Japan

Handmade by Vietnamese craftsmen for Japanese homeware brand Moheim, this mug is finished with a matte exterior while its thin-lipped form makes it a pleasure to drink from.

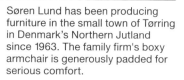

30 SL 60 armchair
Søren Lund, Denmark

Søren Lund has been producing furniture in the small town of Tørring in Denmark's Northern Jutland since 1963. The family firm's boxy armchair is generously padded for serious comfort.

31 Solair chair
*Fabio Fabiano &
Michelange Panzini,
Canada*

A Canadian classic, this plastic and steel chair, available in eye-catching red, green and orange, has been brightening balconies from Montréal to Miami since it appeared on the market in 1972.

32 Stabellenbank bench
Seitz, Switzerland

The hand-turned legs and strong joinery of Swiss industrial designer Kevin Seitz's European-ash bench offer a clean and modern take on the classic seat found in Alpine homes, farms and bars.

33 Fir cuckoo clock
More Trees, Japan

There's something pleasing about marking the passing of time with a cuckoo call. So we're singing the praises of this stripped back Naoto Fukasawa number that celebrates the natural texture of the wood.

34 01 low stool
Maruni, Japan

Jasper Morrison's design for Japanese furniture-maker Maruni offers a flexible seating option. Made of solid maple, its central hole makes it easy to carry and pull up just about anywhere.

35 Kubus KBK 110-50 sink
Franke, Switzerland

This porcelain bowl from Aarburg-based Franke might sink into your benchtop – and sit flush with it too – but its depth and strong lines mean it won't disappear into the background.

36 Bastone cabinet
Poiat, Finland

A rising star in Finland, Antrei Hartikainen's cabinet is both practical and a sculptural art piece. Light filters through the wooden slats, casting playful shadows that contrast with the thicker shelves.

37 Georg clothes hanger
Skagerak, Denmark

Putting on well made clothes is a pleasure and, thanks to this Nordic design, putting them away is too. The flat oak hanger's rounded edges draw on Japanese and Scandinavian aesthetics.

38 Adorawaschen V4000
V-Zug, Switzerland

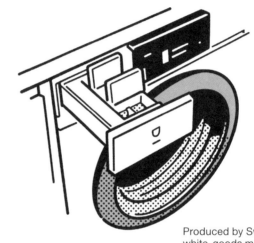

Produced by Switzerland's leading white-goods manufacturer, founded in 1913, the sleek Andorawaschen V4000 is an energy-efficient addition to the laundry room.

39 A Line storage bench III
Form & Refine, Denmark

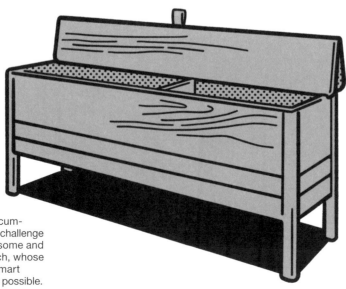

Making beautiful seating-cum-storage is quite the design challenge but Form & Refine's handsome and highly functional oak bench, whose seat can be lifted with a smart leather handle, proves it is possible.

40 Stelz modular system
Eternit, Switzerland

When it comes to indoor plants, the more the merrier. This modular system can be expanded vertically and horizontally, making it a green and versatile addition to any abode.

41 Gränsfors hand hatchet
Gränsfors Bruks, Sweden

Bigger doesn't always mean better. Despite its short handle, this Swedish-made axe can be used for felling small trees and splitting firewood. Who said lumberjacks with chainsaws have all the fun?

42 EA 117 aluminium chair
Vitra, Switzerland

43 Tile throws
Teixidors, Spain

Teixidors began producing loom-woven textiles in Barcelona in 1983. The weaving processes make each piece unique, allowing the raw materials' nuances to reveal themselves in the finished fabric.

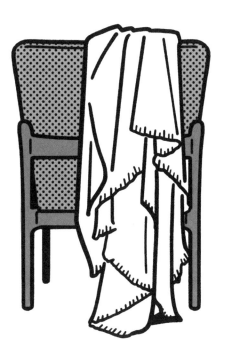

This aluminium and ribbed-leather swivel chair was created for Vitra in 1958 by Charles and Ray Eames. Durable and comfortable, it remains a classic of ergonomic design.

44 Beogram 4000c record player
Bang & Olufsen, Denmark

Jacob Jensen's record player for Bang & Olufsen defined home music when it debuted in the 1970s. A limited edition was reissued in 2020 with a handful of contemporary updates.

45 Oak rotary clothes dryer
Stewi, Switzerland

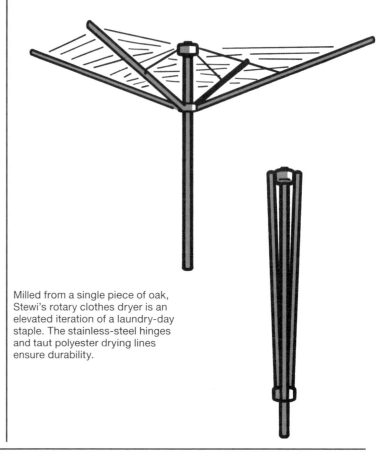

Milled from a single piece of oak, Stewi's rotary clothes dryer is an elevated iteration of a laundry-day staple. The stainless-steel hinges and taut polyester drying lines ensure durability.

46 R40 mirror
Owl, Spain

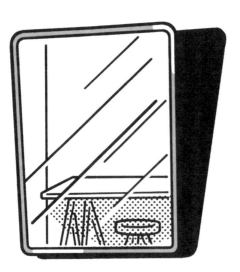

Sebastian Wrong, the British sculptor-turned-designer, first introduced the R40 mirror in 2018. He used newly created wood-sculpting techniques to form the frame's gentle, curved silhouette.

47 Silent drawer cabinet
De Padova, Italy

This handsome, solid oak cabinet is beautifully versatile. Launched in 2020, it is equally at home storing clothes in the bedroom, crockery and utensils in the kitchen or even office supplies in a workspace.

48   Shrub shears 217
Okatsune, Japan

Japan's most popular garden-clippers, these hard-wearing shears are perfect for topiary. The blades are of Izumo Yasugi steel and the soft-grip handles crafted from native oak.

49   MP trolley
Massproductions, Sweden

Conceived by Chris Martin, the British co-founder of Stockholm's Massproductions, this trolley melds circular and angular volumes. The trays are of black-stained oak nestled on a stainless-steel frame.

50   BC03 classic analogue alarm clock
Braun, Germany

Designed by Dietrich Lubs and Dieter Rams in 1987, this piece has undergone various iterations but the simple design of the original makes it the perfect bedmate whether you're travelling or at home.

51   Autumn sofa
Time & Style, Japan

The cushions of this sofa are filled with a surprising material: feathers. The result is splendidly comfortable with what sofa-makers call good "recovery": the seats bounce back however long you lounge.

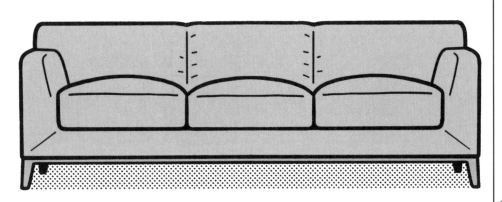

52   Plant pot
Kinto, Japan

The best part of this plastic pot is hidden from view: an interior drainage system that means plants will neither rot nor drip. Kinto has solved the great hanging plant dilemma with style.

53 Four Leaves coat stand
Magis, Italy

Crafted by Barber Osgerby, this stand's four "leaves" each hold a coat, the arms function as mini racks for hangers and the whole things is so attractive it's almost a shame to cover it with a rain jacket.

54 Akademia chair
Nikari, Finland

A combination of Shaker style with Japanese and Finnish design traditions, this lightweight chair comes in ash or oak in various finishes. It can also be upholstered but why gild the lily?

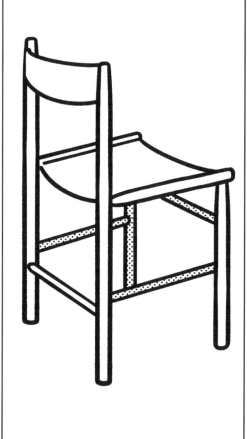

55 Cesta lamp
Santa & Cole, Spain

The wooden Cesta ("basket") lamp is inspired by historic lanterns: the decorative handle allows you to move it easily from room to room. The dimmer switch also means it's usable at all hours.

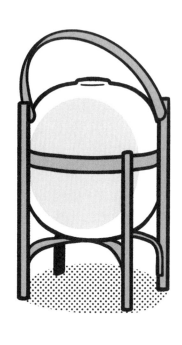

57 Trinkservice No 283 carafe and glasses
Lobmeyr, Austria

56 Cutting board
Breka, Slovenia

Stylish and practical enough to bring to the table, this bread board's deep-toned walnut wood gives it centrepiece status while internal slats mean your table remains crumb-free, even after seconds.

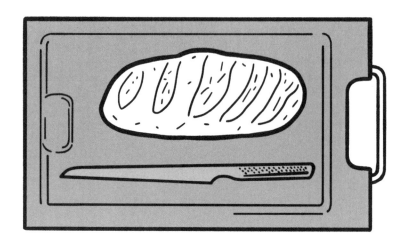

This crystal glassware may have originally been created for Vienna Design Week 2010 but a decade or so is no time at all for Lobmeyr, founded in 1823. The items have changed: the craftsmanship has not.

58 Basic table
Nikari, Finland

Made with renewable energy, this elegant table is the perfect foil to Nikari's Akademia chair. Also available in ash or oak, it's flat-packed, easily assembled and even more easily enjoyed.

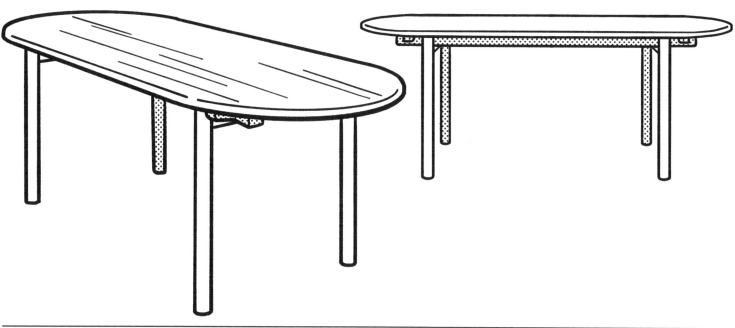

59 Copper coffee caddy
Kaikado, Japan

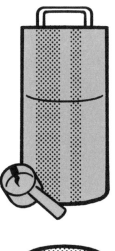

While this caddy protects your coffee from the elements – it's fully airtight – the container's exterior acquires a slight patina over time. That way each of these handmade pieces ends up being subtly unique.

60 Domo floor lamp
Karakter Copenhagen, Denmark

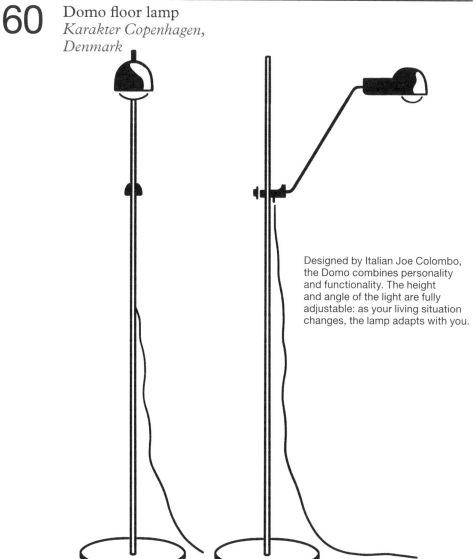

Designed by Italian Joe Colombo, the Domo combines personality and functionality. The height and angle of the light are fully adjustable: as your living situation changes, the lamp adapts with you.

61 Piazzino easy parasol
Glatz, Switzerland

62 MC20 Cugino stool/table
Mattiazzi, Italy

Fashioned from solid oak, the Konstantin Grcic-designed Cugino stool – which doubles as a side table – excels at the classic but surprisingly rare feat of being as functional as it is well formed.

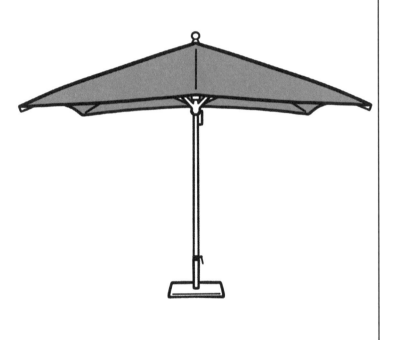

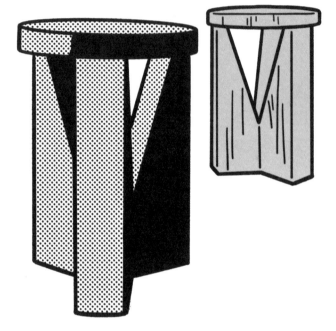

Glatz has kept the Swiss cool since 1895 and the compact and user-friendly Piazzino easy parasol is the laidback bestseller that will throw shade for many seasons.

63 PC desk
Pacific Furniture Service, Japan

64 Four-piece place setting
Monoware, UK

Handmade in Tokyo, this birch-beauty of a desk – specifically created for working on a computer – renders the home office a far more elegant and enjoyable affair.

British brand Monoware makes ceramics that are meticulously designed but as simple as possible: this pared-down set will reliably and stylishly serve all your dinner party needs.

65 Palissade chaise longue
Hay, Denmark

As an outdoor lounger, Hay's Palissade is the perfect all-rounder: it is comfy to recline on when the sun shines, hardy enough to withstand cold winters and looks chic on the patio whatever the weather.

66 Wine-o bottle rack
Wireworks, UK

This rack includes wall fixtures and a clever interlocking mechanism making it customisable to any space and collection. Made from natural oak, it is a deserving holder of even the most treasured vintages.

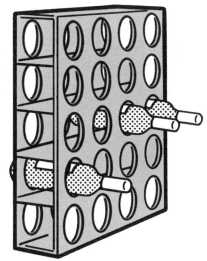

67 365+ carafe
Ikea, Sweden

68 Tiiliskivi tablecloth
Marimekko, Finland

Sitting at the more muted end of the scale when it comes to pieces by legacy textile house Marimekko, the Tiiliskivi tablecloth (the name means "brick" in Finnish) will complement almost any table setting.

With its clean design, practical cork stopper and very budget-friendly price tag, it is no surprise that Ikea's 365+ glass carafe has become a standard feature in homes across Scandinavia – and beyond.

69 Camaleonda sofa
B&B Italia, Italy

Thanks to its pioneering modularity, this icon of 1970s Italian interior design by Mario Bellini can be positioned in a snug corner or as a striking centrepiece – and you can always change your mind later.

70 Pottery pitcher
Another Country, UK

When it comes to items for daily use, simpler is often better. This pitcher by Brit favourite Another Country is handmade from white stoneware and clear glazed for an understated and refined finish.

71 Functional Form+ cutting set
Fiskars, Finland

The oldest company in Finland, established in 1649, Fiskars crafts practical items like this kitchen cutting set, made with high-quality Japanese stainless steel and sculpted handles for comfort.

72 Federzugleuchte spring balanced lamp
Midgard, Germany

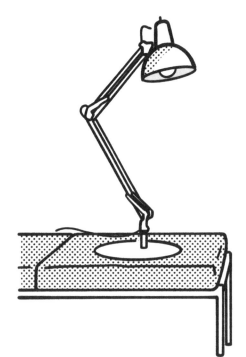

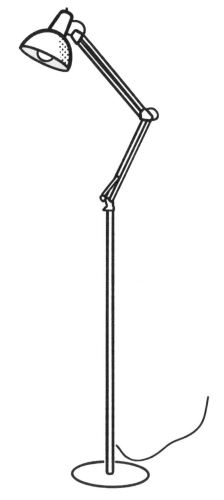

Midgard was relaunched in 2017, reviving the timeless lamps designed by Curt Fischer in the 1920s. The classic Federzugleuchte is available as a table, wall, ceiling or floor lamp and is an illuminating choice.

73 Case Study cylinder with stand
Modernica, USA

Handmade in LA, Modernica's stoneware planters are a stylish option for bringing a bit of greenery into your home. The four-legged stand comes in teak or powder-coated steel.

74 Hotaru Marker table light lamp
Ozeki & Co, Japan

Manufactured in rural Gifu using centuries-old techniques, this lamp, featuring translucent bark paper stretched over a bamboo structure, emits a soft glow like the Japanese firefly it takes its name from.

75 D.552.2 coffee table
Molteni & C, Italy

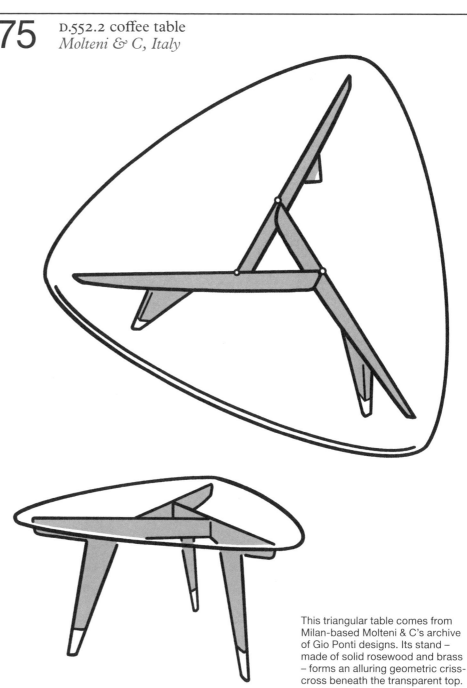

This triangular table comes from Milan-based Molteni & C's archive of Gio Ponti designs. Its stand – made of solid rosewood and brass – forms an alluring geometric criss-cross beneath the transparent top.

76 Tower toothbrush stand
Yamazaki, Japan

Japanese brand Yamazaki makes common household items with a focus on simplicity. This stand can hold up to six toothbrushes and a tube of toothpaste, keeping the bathroom looking spick and span.

77 Kitchen Tower unit
Peka, Switzerland

Peka specialises in efficient storage. This pull-out kitchen unit has special sections for knives, wooden spoons and cutting boards to ensure the counter remains clutter-free.

78 Roller cabinet
A Petersen, Denmark

Knud Holscher designed this cabinet like "a vertical version of the travel trunk". Initially intended for office use, it later found its natural home in Holscher's kitchen, storing spices, plates and pans.

79 Loop coffee table
Isokon Plus, UK

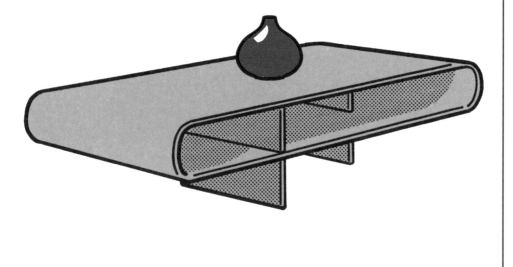

The curved Loop coffee table, created for Isokon Plus in 1996, can be found in the permanent collections of the Metropolitan Museum of Art in New York and the Victoria & Albert Museum in London.

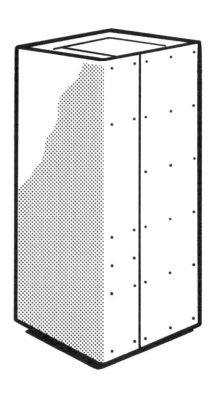

80 Spaghetti outdoor armchair
Fiam, Italy

The Spaghetti deckchair is almost as ubiquitous in Italy as the pasta it's named after. Reminiscent of 1960s beach holidays, it includes a comfortable footrest and comes in several sunny colours.

81 Holocene No 1 oil lamp
Wästberg, Sweden

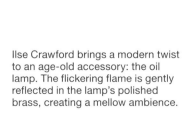

Ilse Crawford brings a modern twist to an age-old accessory: the oil lamp. The flickering flame is gently reflected in the lamp's polished brass, creating a mellow ambience.

82 Teapot
Hasami, Japan

Hasami Porcelain's squat, stackable teapot – designed in LA and manufactured in Japan – is made from a traditional mix of porcelain and clay, giving it an earthy and warm texture.

83 Pride stainless steel cutlery set
David Mellor, UK

Mid-century British designer David Mellor created this understated, slimline cutlery set in 1953, which remains a modern classic to this day. Proof that it's not just what you eat, it's *how* you eat that counts.

84 FK sofa
Truck Furniture, Japan

Truck's soft corduroy sofa is immediately inviting. Its design is laidback and generous, with ample armrests and plump pillows making it a perfect spot for lazy afternoons or cosy evenings.

85 Bathroom A shelving
String Furniture, Sweden

Sweden's modular String shelving, with its unmistakable aesthetic, has been providing an understated backdrop for everything from books and plants to bathroom accessories since 1949.

86 Glass French press
Yield, USA

This cafetière is made from heat-proof borosilicate glass, which looks delicate but is reassuringly strong. The shapely copper pull adds a smart finish to a fresh take on the classic press.

87 LS 990 metal light switch
Jung, Germany

The simple LS 990 light switch is admired for its clean lines and generously sized boxy rocker, which comes in the same material as the frame and responds to the gentlest touch.

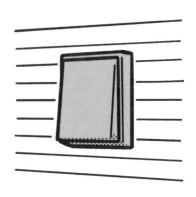

88 Sonar washbasin
Laufen, Switzerland

Patricia Urquiola's washbasin for Laufen melds functionality with playfulness. Her curvy creations are made possible thanks to the brand's SaphirKeramik – a strong yet pliable ceramic material.

89 Willow bed
Jardan, Australia

Jardan furniture nods to Australia's modernist heritage. The Willow bed is no exception, bringing together tactile rattan in its rounded headboard with a solid base made from American oak.

91 Library lamp
Andreas Martin Löf, Sweden

Originally designed for Monocle in 2012, Stockholm-based architect Andreas Martin Löf gives a clever twist to the traditional bookend by combining a folded metal body with a light holder.

90 Washlet RX Ewater+
Toto, Japan

This streamlined, hi-tech toilet is a real people pleaser: think heated seats and all sorts of sprays and jets to keep discerning derrières – and itself – squeaky clean.

92 Kyoto table
Poltrona Frau, Italy

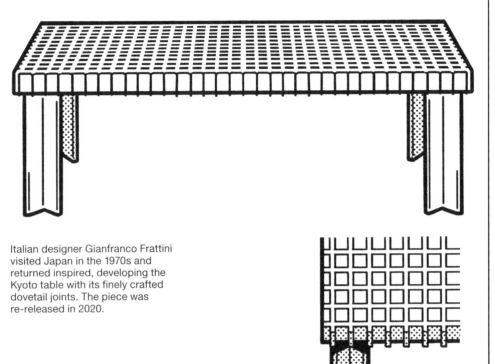

Italian designer Gianfranco Frattini visited Japan in the 1970s and returned inspired, developing the Kyoto table with its finely crafted dovetail joints. The piece was re-released in 2020.

93 Kobenstyle casserole
Dansk, Denmark

Created in 1956 by Danish sculptor Jens Quistgaard, this fiery red casserole dish is made from sturdy enamelware and features a practical lid handle that doubles as a trivet.

94 Essence white wine glass
Iittala, Finland

Part of Iittala's award-winning Essence drinkware collection, these elegant wine glasses designed by Zürich-based Alfredo Häberli bring a touch of Finnish simplicity and functionality to the dinner table.

95 Normandie cushion cover
Johanna Gullichsen, Finland

Made with traditional Finnish weaving techniques, Helsinki designer Joanna Gullichsen blends her signature modern patterns with earthy Scandinavian tones in these double-sided cotton cushion covers.

96 Cartesio bathtub
Agape, Italy

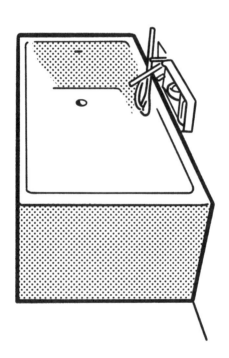

This simple freestanding bathtub, made of soft stone-like material and conceived by Italian collective Benedini Associati, combines sophisticated geometric lines with built-in storage space.

97 EM77 kettle
Stelton, Denmark

A classic of Danish kitchenware, the Erik Magnussen-designed EM77 jug first appeared as a thermos in the 1970s and is now available as a kettle.

98 Haller system
USM, Switzerland

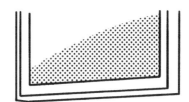

USM's bespoke modular shelving system has been furnishing offices since 1965. Built with meticulous Swiss precision, it can be configured in myriad ways and is available in varying tones.

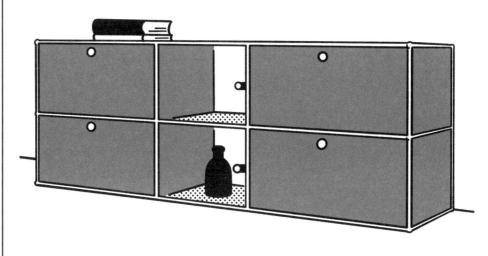

99 Ceiling lamp No 1
Muller van Severen, Belgium

Created as a singular bent and lacquered steel tube, this ceiling lamp adds playfulness to any room and is the first of many collaborative designs by Belgian duo Muller van Severen.

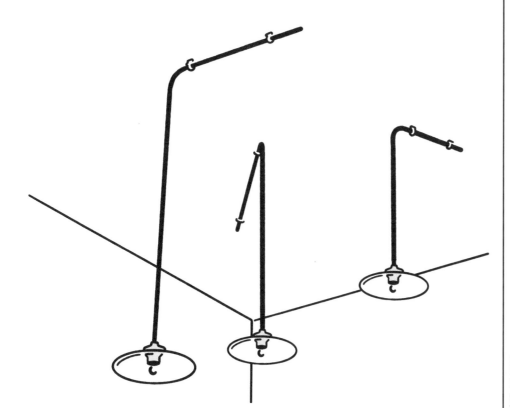

100 Utensil holder
Permanent Collection, UK

Hand-crafted by woodworkers in northeastern Slovenia, this handsome utensil holder with its clean hexagonal form is carved from pear and walnut wood sourced from local orchards.

About Monocle
Magazine and more

In 2007, MONOCLE was launched as a monthly magazine briefing on global affairs, business, design and more. Today we have a thriving print business, a radio station, shops, cafés, books, films and events. At our core is the simple belief that there will always be a place for a brand that is committed to telling fresh stories, delivering good journalism and being on the ground around the world. We're Zürich and London-based and have bureaux in Hong Kong, Tokyo, Los Angeles and Toronto. Over the years our editors and correspondents have learnt how to make the most of a living space. This knowledge is unpacked in this book and throughout our reporting on Monocle 24, in film on our website and, of course, across our print and digital products.

For more information head to *monocle.com*

Monocle magazine

MONOCLE magazine is published 10 times a year, including two double issues (July/August and December/January). We also have annual specials: THE FORECAST and two editions of THE ENTREPRENEURS. Look out for our seasonal weekly newspapers too.

Monocle 24 radio

Our round-the-clock internet radio station delivers global news and shows covering foreign affairs, urbanism, business, culture, food and drink, design and print media. You can listen live or download from *monocle.com/radio* – or wherever you get your podcasts.

Books

Since 2013, MONOCLE has been publishing books like this one, which follows in the footsteps of our best-selling titles *The Monocle Book of Italy* and *The Monocle Book of Gentle Living*. All our books are available on our site, through our distributor Thames & Hudson or at all good book shops.

Monocle Minute

MONOCLE's smartly appointed family of newsletters come from our team of editors and bureaux chiefs around the world. From the daily Monocle Minute to the Monocle Weekend Edition and our weekly On Design special, sign up to get the latest in lifestyle, affairs and design, straight to your inbox every day.

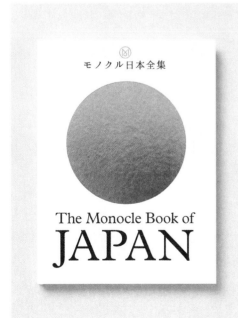

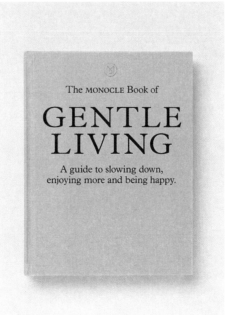

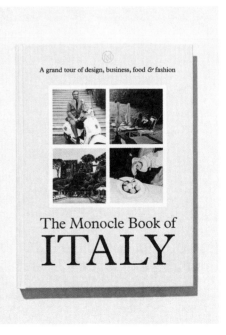

Index

Acknowledgements

The Monocle Book of Homes

EDITORS
Nolan Giles
Joe Pickard

DESIGNER
Sam Brogan

PHOTO EDITORS
Matthew Beaman
Shin Miura
Lucy Pullicino

PRODUCTION
Jacqueline Deacon

Special thanks:
Emily Nathan
Amy Richardson
Chris Yeo

Researchers:
Gabriele Dellisanti
Arisa Sigrist
Julia Webster Ayuso
Zayana Zulkiflee

Writers:
Liam Aldous
Hamish Anderson
Kimberly Bradley
Tyler Brûlé
Petri Burtsoff
Mario de Castro
Zoe Chan Eayrs
Gianfranco Chicco
Adrian Craddock
Ilse Crawford
Gabriele Dellisanti
Tishani Doshi
Lucinda Elliott
Josh Fehnert
Lia Forslund
Nolan Giles
Georgina Godwin
Sophie Grove
Rolf Hay
Daphné Hézard
Morten Hjortshøj
Daphne Karnezis
Tomos Lewis
Liv Lewitschnik
Nic Monisse
Byron Peart
Dexter Peart
Joe Pickard
Patrick Pittman
David Plaisant
Molly Price
Tom Reynolds
Andrew Romano
Stella Roos
Florian Siebeck
Arisa Sigrist
Pan Siripark
Aisha Speirs
Richard Spencer Powell
Ed Stocker
Lou Stoppard
Andrew Tuck
Hester Underhill
Julia Webster Ayuso
Fiona Wilson
Sonia Zhuravlyova

Photographers:
Alex Atack
Yves Bachmann
Monica Barreneche
Felix Brüggemann
Sharyn Cairns
Gaia Cambiaggi
David Chatfield
Jesse Chehak
Adib Chowdhury
Ana Cuba
DePasquale+Maffini
Tishani Doshi
Evelyn Dragan
Åke E:son Lindman
Leo Fabrizio
Sean Fennessy
Luigi Fiano
Joe Fletcher
Michael Gannon
Dan Glasser
Jenny Gustafsson
Marnie Hawson
Benya Hegenbarth
Jose Hevia
Tina Hillier
Ross Honeysett
Ana Hop
Lauryn Ishak
Lek Kiatsirikajorn
Bart Kiggen
Younès Klouche
Nelson Kon
Liz Kuball
Juho Kuva
Mark Kushimi
Lindsay Lauckner Gundlock
Salva López
Tony Luong
Ehrin Macksey
Lea Meienberg
Trevor Mein
Shin Miura
James Mollison
Andrew L Moore
Fram Parente
Ian Patterson
Zara Pfeiffer
Tim O'Connor
Felix Odell

Koichiro Ogasahara
Benjamin Quinton
Benjamin Rasmussen
Joel Redman
Markel Redondo
Tuca Reinés
Robert Rieger
Tom Ross
Toby Scott
Ben Shaw
Guillaume Simoneau
Jan Søndergaard
Edmund Sumner
Kohei Take
Polly Tootal
Eirini Vourloumis
Martin Westlake
Dan Wilton
Marvin Zilm

Images:
Alamy
Getty Images
Magnum Photos
Petr Polák

Illustrator:
Ryo Kaneyasu

Monocle

EDITORIAL DIRECTOR
& CHAIRMAN
Tyler Brûlé

EDITOR IN CHIEF
Andrew Tuck

CREATIVE DIRECTOR
Richard Spencer Powell

BOOKS EDITOR
Joe Pickard

DEPUTY EDITOR
Molly Price

ASSISTANT EDITOR
Hester Underhill

DESIGNERS
Sam Brogan
Maria Hamer
Giulia Tugnoli

PHOTO EDITORS
Matthew Beaman
Shin Miura
Lucy Pullicino

PRODUCTION
Jacqueline Deacon

Thank you